A HISTORY OF
DALTON-IN-FURNESS

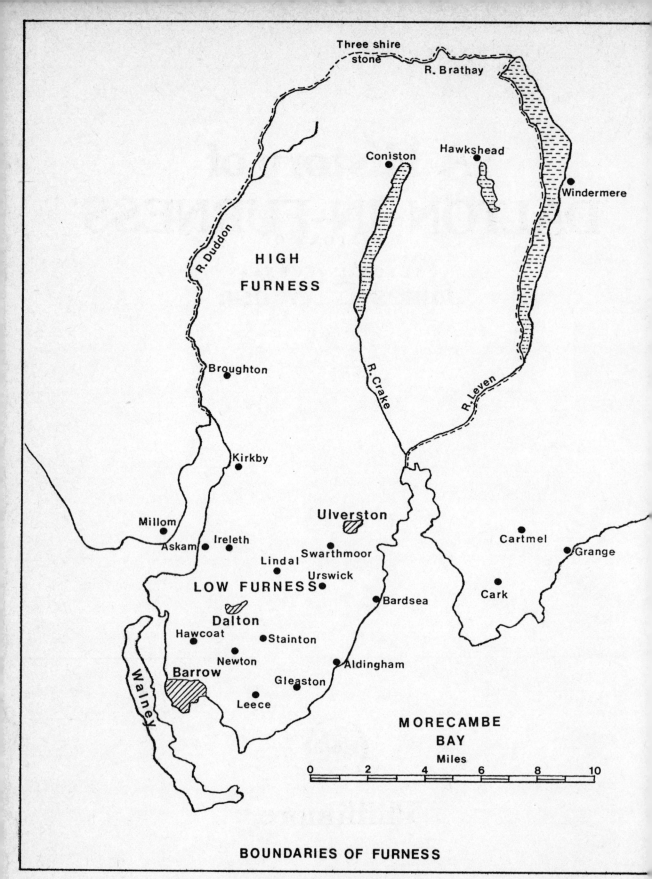

The boundaries of Furness.

A History of
DALTON~IN~FURNESS

James E. Walton

Phillimore

1984

Published by
PHILLIMORE & CO. LTD.
Shopwyke Hall, Chichester, Sussex

ISBN 0 85033 517 5

Typeset in the United Kingdom by
Fidelity Processes - Selsey - Sussex

Printed and bound in Great Britain by
THE CAMELOT PRESS LTD
Southampton, England

CONTENTS

LIST OF TEXT ILLUSTRATIONS

LIST OF PLATES

(between pages 50 and 51)

INTRODUCTION

Amateur local historians are by no means a rare species. They can be found in all walks of life, and be of almost any age; but one thing they all have in common is curiosity — a desire to know more about the past, whether it be last year or a thousand years ago. Their involvement in the subject may be deep and earnest, or it may merely be an appreciation of the importance of photographing a decaying row of buildings before the demolition men move in. Both are important, for tomorrow, today will be history.

My curiosity was aroused in 1967 following a conversation with an acquaintance who was keenly interested in the town's history. I did not know it then, but this friendly chat was completely to alter the course of my life, and ultimately resulted in the publication of my first book on the history of Dalton, in 1972. This first publication left much to be desired, and in view of this, I decided to start again and try to produce a better, more comprehensive history of the town. To what extent I have succeeded in this only you, the reader, will be able to decide. I have included references wherever possible, and, for ease of reading, these are principally contained within the text. For obvious reasons I cannot claim that everything in the following pages is accurate and correct. Many assumptions have been made in the light of the available evidence; but, where doubt exists, I have tried to indicate this in the text.

Obviously this is only a general history, and a great deal of information has had to be left out. Many of the individual topics in the following pages are worthy of more detailed study, and if this book serves to stimulate the interest of the reader, and create a desire to discover more, then its purpose will have been fulfilled.

Dalton
1984

JAMES E. WALTON

ACKNOWLEDGEMENTS

During the preparation of this book, I have had to enlist the help of many people, and in every case I was gratified and encouraged by the enthusiastic and helpful response I received to my enquiries. Without this invaluable assistance my task would have been much more difficult, if not impossible. Although there are too many people involved for me to mention them all by name, I would particularly like to thank the following, and apologise to all those whose names are not mentioned.

Mr. Ernest Boddy, Mr. Allan Cassley, Mr. James Melville, O.B.E., Mr. Tom Quirk, all of whom helped in various ways. Mr. Ivan Whitehead, for allowing me ready access to newspapers, documents etc. in the castle; Mr. Owen Osmotherley, for photographic assistance; the late Miss June Nelson, for the loan of books; Nora Marshall, for many hours spent collecting information; Mrs. Margaret Copley and the late Bill Edwards for their reminiscences; Mrs. Jan Matthews and Mrs. Christine Martin for assistance with typing; Mrs. Sheana Bark for information about the Town Band. In particular I would like to thank Brett Harrison, late Archivist-in-Charge, Public Record Office, Barrow, for much valuable assistance, and offer my sincere apologies for the non-inclusion of his excellent written contribution on the Mills of the Ancient Parish of Dalton — a factor only determined by the need to abbreviate my original manuscript. For the same reason I must also tender my sincere thanks and apologies to Harry Kellett, Paul Gilbert and Sam Thompson. Thanks are also due to Ron Smith, Alan Boulton and other members of the staff of the Reference Library, Barrow, for their kind assistance, and to Jonathan Wignall, whose extensive knowledge of local mining was of immense value. Finally, I would like to thank the Barrow-in-Furness Borough Council for permission to include extracts from *Barrow & District* by F. Barnes, Mr. Russell Rowlandson for allowing me to quote from William Fisher's diary, and Dr. William Rollinson, of the University of Liverpool, Institute of Extension Studies, for all his help and encouragement.

Acknowledgements for Illustrations

I should like to thank Cumbria County Council Record Office for permission to reproduce plates nos. 1 and 2; Barrow Reference Library for nos. 3, 8, 10, 15, 16, 18 and 19; Ivan Whitehead for nos. 17, 22, 30 and 33; R. J. Hartley for nos. 20, 21 and 23; Mrs. D. Corbett for nos. 28, 31, 32, 36 and 37; Dalton Fire Brigade for no. 34; R. J. Foxon for no. 35; and Mr. T. Quirk for no. 26.

My thanks are equally due to the Ordnance Survey for permission to use one of their maps as the basis for the second text illustration (Crown Copyright Reserved); Barrow Library for permission to reproduce nos. 5 and 15; the Revd. Trevor Park for no. 7; Jonathan Wignall for no. 13; Ernest Boddy for no. 19; the *Dalton Guardian* for no. 27; and Cumbria County Council Record Office for the use of maps on which nos. 3 and 28 are based.

To the people of Dalton-in-Furness

Chapter One

EARLY HISTORY

Situation

THE FURNESS[1] PENINSULA is situated in the north-west corner of England, marking what was previously the northern extremity of the county of Lancashire, but is now, since the reorganisation of local government in 1974, the southernmost tip of Cumbria. The northern part of Furness lies in the Lakeland hills and is known as High Furness or Furness Fells, and is almost completely bounded by water from the river Duddon and its estuary in the west, and the Brathay, Lake Windermere, the Leven and Morecambe Bay on the east. The southernmost part of Furness is bounded by the sea and is known as Low or Plain Furness.

The town of Dalton is situated near the centre of Low Furness on the eastern crest of a glacial valley which runs obliquely across the peninsula. Just over a mile to the south in another part of this valley (which was anciently known as Bekansgill, and more recently as the Vale of Nightshade) stand the picturesque ruins of Furness Abbey, a place which had a profound effect on the history and development of Dalton. The isolation of this corner of the country was also an important factor in the economic development of Furness, into which the only means of access, other than by sea, was through the hills and forests of High Furness or the hazardous route across the sands at low tide.

In the beginning: prehistoric evidence

Although time has almost completely obscured all precise knowledge of the dim and distant past in Furness, sufficient evidence exists in the form of earthworks and artefacts to tell us that man has existed here for many thousands of years, and that this remote corner of the country was already steeped in history when the Romans came to Britain almost 2,000 years ago. Stone axes, adzes and hammers in various stages of completion have been discovered in Furness, principally on Walney Island, but also at High Haume (Ordnance Survey map reference 226760) and many other parts of the peninsula. The fact that so many of these artefacts were unfinished strongly suggests that they were made here, but local opinion favours the idea that the Furness sites were not permanently occupied throughout the year, and that the stone from which these implements were manufactured was brought here from elsewhere, probably Langdale. The museum at Barrow possesses a considerable collection of locally discovered Stone Age artefacts.

1

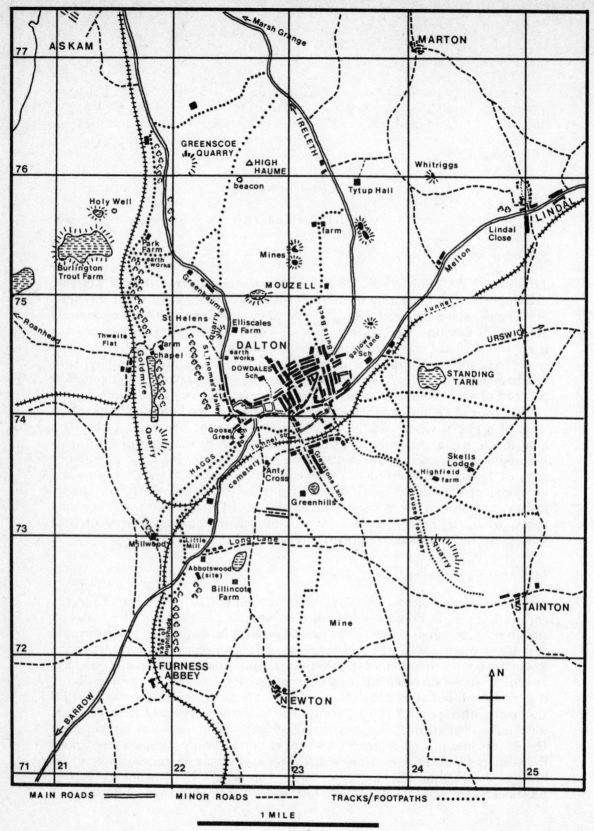

1. Map of area around Dalton.

The following labels appear on the map:

ASKAM

77

Marsh Grange

MARTON

76

GREENSCOE QUARRY

△HIGH HAUME

IRELETH

Whitriggs

beacon

Tytup Hall

Holy Well

farm

LINDAL

Park Farm

earth works

Mines

Lindal Close

Burlington Trout Farm

Greenhaume

Melton

MOUZELL

75

Roanhead

St Helens

Ellescales Farm

Butts Beck

tunnel

URSWICK

Thwaite Flat

farm chapel

DALTON

earth works

gallows Sch land

Goldmire

St.Thomas's Valley

DOWDALES Sch

STANDING TARN

74

Quarry

HAGGS

Goose Green

Tunnel

Skells Lodge

Highfield farm

cemetery

Anty Cross

Gleaston Lane

disused railway

quarry

Greenhills

73

Millwood

Little Mill

Long Lane

Abbotswood (site)

Billincote Farm

STAINTON

Mine

72

Vale of Nightshade

FURNESS ABBEY

△N

BARROW

NEWTON

71

21   22   23   24   25

MAIN ROADS ———   MINOR ROADS -------   TRACKS/FOOTPATHS ·······

1 MILE

Even at this remote time a primitive form of technology evolved, and the progression from stone to copper and bronze was inevitable. The fact that we have discovered fewer Bronze Age artefacts than those made from stone in no way suggests a decline in population at this time; it is because of the fact that these metals corrode as a result of chemical activity, and, after being buried for countless centuries in damp soil can disappear completely. Some relics of this era did, however, survive. Two corroded copper weapons, believed to have been battle-axes, were discovered sometime before 1805 just to the west of the town, on the Haggs. Unfortunately they have both since disappeared, having been either lost or destroyed; but without doubt the most important and interesting Bronze Age discoveries at Dalton occurred almost simultaneously in the year 1874, when quarrying operations at Butts Beck (233747) and Goldmire (218738) revealed the burial places of two warriors. As may be expected, the workmen who made these discoveries were ignorant of their true value, with predictably disastrous results as may be see from the following descriptions. The *Ulverston Mirror*, 24 October 1874, reports:

Within the last few days the discovery of a skeleton at Goldmire Quarry, near Dalton, has given rise to some little speculation . . . Cutting down the brow of the hill by degrees caused the bones to fall with the stones a few at a time. The whole of the bones were placed in a wheelbarrow before Mr. Jackson was informed of the event which was on Friday, or that gentleman would have had the top of the hill properly bared, so as to procure the skeleton perfect . . . a sword in a scabbard was found with the remains of this warrior. Difficulty was experienced in collecting the remains, as various portions were carried to Dalton, whilst the sword was broken into pieces, which were taken by the workpeople as mementoes or relics . . .

The following account refers to the discovery at Bucks Beck, and was reported in the *Proceedings of the Barrow Naturalists' Field Club*, Volume XVII:

When found, the vault was covered by a large limestone slab and was 6 feet long, 4 feet deep and nearly 4 feet wide . . . At one end was found a bronze spearhead, and at the other, a bronze sword. When the vault was first opened, the weapons appeared to be in quite a good state of preservation, but soon, on exposure to the atmosphere, the hilt and guard of the sword crumbled into a powder. The blade of the sword was slightly bent and when one of the workmen tried to straighten it, he only succeeded in breaking it in two . . .

There were so many points of similarity between these two burials that one could be excused for thinking that only one discovery had been made and that it had been incorrectly reported; but the fundamental differences (i.e. the location and type of burial), combined with the fact that both sources must be considered reliable precludes this observation.

Mining activity in the 19th century and intensive agriculture have certainly obliterated many earthworks around the town, but some have survived. At High Haume, one of the possible sites of Hougun (*see* p. 7), a circular enclosure is easily discernible from the ground, and, although nothing is known of its history, it is quite possible that it was in some way associated with the beacon which once existed here. Aerial photography reveals other earthworks at

Housethwaite Hill near Park Farm (218753), and at Elliscales (225745). Nothing is known about either of these two sites, but the possibility that they only date from the Middle Ages must not be discounted.

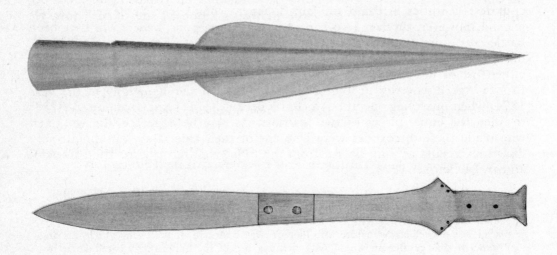

2. Bronze spearhead and sword found at Butts Beck in 1874. The blade of the sword has been broken, and was repaired by means of a bronze plate rivetted on. Both these weapons are now in the Lancaster Museum.

As far as the history of Dalton is concerned, however, the earthworks which formerly existed in the churchyard are of special interest, for it is reasonably certain that this is where the old town was born. Situated on a hillside plateau, with the ground falling steeply away on three sides and a nearby stream providing a convenient supply of water, this was an excellent site for defence, a point which will be referred to later. Firstly, however, we must look at these earthworks a little more closely. In 1850, whilst an extension to the churchyard was being made, the ground was levelled and all traces of these earthworks were erased, so now we can only rely upon contemporary accounts by two local historians of the 18th and 19th centuries, describing in one case the site, and in the other an excavation of the earthworks.

Father Thomas West was a Jesuit priest and historian who lived at Tytup Hall (236759) in the 1770s. It was while residing there that he wrote his memorable book *Antiquities of Furness*, which was published in 1775. Father West was convinced that these earthworks marked the site of a Roman fort built in A.D. 79 by Agricola as he advanced northwards through Britain, and he went to great lengths to identify Morecambe Bay[2] with the place of the same name mentioned by Ptolemy (A.D. 90–168) during an exploration of the western coastline of Britain. He then tells us that Tacitus, Agricola's son-in-law, described the contemplated crossing of the Morecambe estuary as being the most dangerous of the five between the rivers Dee and Duddon. This would appear to support West's theory that the Romans did enter Furness, and if they followed the ancient route across the peninsula they would certainly pass through Dalton, with the road taking them very close to West's supposed site of their fort. He says of this site:

> ...The area of the castellum has probably been all the churchyard, the ground on which the present castle stands, and from that to the crest of the precipice on the western side. The situation is such as Agricola would have made choice of, and such as the Romans always did make choice of, where it was possible. Steep rocks on the southern and a precipice on the western side, with a rampart and ditch on the eastern secured the fort from surprise ...

The following description of the earthworks was written by William Close (see p. 86), a surgeon and local historian, at the beginning of the 19th century:

> ...On the east side of the churchyard there is a long hollow which has the appearance of a defensive ditch, backed by a mound of earth resembling the remains of a rampart. These have been frequently supposed to be the remains of outworks formed for the defence of a garrison placed here by Agricola to secure the conquest of Furness. As no remains of Roman antiquity, however, were ever known to have been found near the place, we were desirous to examine the materials of which the mound is formed, in order to determine whether it was natural, or had been raised by human industry. ... The vicar having obligingly given permission, that any part of the premises might be examined, three openings were made in different parts of the rampart.
>
> (1) On the east side of the ditch in the churchyard, an irregular foundation of a wall three feet in thickness, consisting of stones without mortar, was found under a quantity of superficial materials.
>
> (2) In the garden near the south end of the rampart, at five or six feet below the surface, immediately under a bed of small, loose pebbles, there was a stratum of dark earth mixed with marine shells.
>
> (3) In a part of the garden opposite the east end of the church, at the depth of six feet below the surface, the soil was mixed with the shells of periwinkles. ... From different circumstances observed in making these perforations, it appeared evident that this mound of earth had been amassed in a great measure by human industry: but for what purpose it was not possible to discover ...

Thus wrote William Close many years ago, and as the results of his excavations yielded no positive proof of Roman occupation we can only assume that, unless the site had been remorselessly pillaged for building materials to such an extent that it became totally unrecognisable, then no Roman fort of any importance ever stood here. Indeed it is generally believed today that the Romans never occupied Furness, and that this site was an Iron Age settlement, similar to that at Castle Hill at Pennington.

The early growth of the town

Even though the almost insular seclusion of Furness must have afforded the inhabitants some measure of isolation from the constant state of unrest which prevailed throughout the rest of Britain, the arrival of the Roman legions in the first century A.D. affected everyone. Although no-one can presume to speak with any degree of certainty about details, the general picture is reasonably clear. The struggle for overlordship which had persisted between the various tribes finally resolved itself in this corner of the country at least with the most powerful of all, the Brigantes, emerging as victors. They, in turn were subjugated by Agricola as he rapidly advanced northwards, and for about four hundred years Roman law prevailed.

In the fifth century, after the Romans had departed, a state of lawlessness and confusion returned to Britain. The north-western coastline was raided almost at will by the Irish, Picts and Scots, and for the isolated communities living in Furness, this period must have been one of constant worry and distress. As well as the forementioned troublemakers, the population of Low Furness also had the fearsome Norsemen to contend with, and it is generally believed that it was because of this coastal piracy that many people deserted their isolated farmsteads near the coast, and moved inland, with the fortified vill of Dalton as their obvious choice. In this way the town of Dalton was born.

Although there can be no doubt that for many years before they actually settled in Furness, the Vikings had raided our coasts with their legendary ferocity, it is quite likely that when they eventually migrated here they came as fugitives, not as conquerors. This would have been about A.D. 895, at which time they were resident in the Isle of Man and had presumed to seek independence from their Norwegian king, who promptly despatched a punitive expedition to quell this revolt and restore his authority in the island.[3] Some indication that these mutinous Norsemen came to our shores seeking sanctuary is apparent in the mixture of Norse and Anglian place names in Furness, suggesting that they came here peacefully and established their own communities alongside those of the natives. They brought their traditions and customs too, and one which lingered long in Furness was the funeral custom of *arval*[4] in which a meal of bread, cheese and ale was provided at the funeral house, and after the interment the parish clerk announced at the graveside the name of the appointed inn to which the mourners were to proceed. There they sat in groups of four and each group was served with two quarts of ale. Half the price of this was paid by the conductor of the funeral, and the other half by the mourners themselves. While the ale was being drunk, each guest was served with a cake called an 'arval cake', to take home to the women and others who could not attend the funeral. Obviously *arval* funerals were expensive and not everyone was buried according to this custom. Nevertheless the tradition had persisted in Dalton for 1,000 years or more, and the last *arval* funeral in the town was that of Mr. James Jackson, a farmer, who died on 25 February, 1849.

Looking back at this remote period, it is difficult to say with any degree of certainty just who the occupants of Furness were at any particular time, but by studying the place names, it seems clear that at various times, the peninsula was colonised by British, Anglian and Norse settlers. According to Barnes (*Barrow & District*), Dalton and Ulverston can both claim an Anglian origin.

In the year 1086, the Domesday survey was completed, and this gives us our earliest documentary information. This part of Furness was in the manor of Hougun and had belonged to the Earls of Northumbria since the time of Canute, and is entered in the survey under 'Agemundreness' (Amounderness), then part of the West Riding of Yorkshire. What information there is is very sketchy, and merely gives a list of manors with a note describing how they were taxed under Edward the Confessor. The following extract is taken from *Barrow & District* by F. Barnes:

> The entry in Domesday Book covering Hougun refers to the time when it was held by Tostig, about 1060, and reads as follows 'In HOUGUN (High Haume) Manor, Earl Tosti had four carucates of land rateable to the geld (i.e. Danegeld). In CHILUESTREUIC (Killerwick) three car., SOUREBI (Sowerby) three car., HIETUN (Hawcoat) four car., DALTUNE (Dalton) two car., WARTE (Thwaite Flat) two car'.

This brief reference marks the end of the era of unrecorded history in Furness, and the beginning of a new era when documentary evidence enables us to identify people, places and events with a greater degree of accuracy. One final comment must be made however about this period; it concerns Hougun, the legendary home of Tosti Godwinson, the Saxon earl, and lord of a large manor which included Dalton and much of Low Furness.

There is now no trace of the former capital of Furness, and we can only speculate on the slenderest of evidence where it might have been. Millom, Urswick and High Haume have all been suggested as possible sites, but it is generally believed today that Millom and Urswick can be discounted. Quite close to High Haume, however, about three-quarters of a mile to the north-west of Dalton Castle, there is an area of high ground known locally as 'Oosteds' (222748), which appears to possess all the right physical features which one would expect to find at the site of an ancient settlement. The name itself is significant, and is almost certainly a centuries-old slang derivation of 'House-steads', a name which strongly suggests the existence of an ancient settlement. However, as mentioned earlier, this is pure speculation, and the chances are that the quest for Hougun will never be satisfactorily concluded.

Chapter Two

THE MIDDLE AGES

The Founding of Furness Abbey

AFTER WILLIAM THE CONQUEROR had been crowned king of England at Westminster on 25 December 1066, the next five years were spent in subjugating the rebellious inhabitants, particularly in the north of the country which was mercilessly devastated. Despite its remoteness, Furness did not escape the Norman onslaught and considerable areas of land were laid waste, and presumably many of its inhabitants put to the sword. At this time, Furness belonged to Roger de Poictou, a Norman lord, and had been granted to him as a reward for services rendered to William during the Conquest; but because he opposed the succession to the throne of Henry — William's third son — Roger was banished from the kingdom, and his possessions in Furness were bestowed upon Stephen, Earl of Boulogne and afterwards King of England.

Although the Normans were fierce warriors, they were also superstitious, and believed they could help to guarantee the safety of their souls by means of generous donations of property and land to the monasteries. In 1127, Stephen, unashamedly admitting his motive, gave part of his 'forest of Furness' to Ewan d'Avranches, abbot of a small Benedictine monastery at Tulketh near Preston. The only land in Low Furness excluded from Stephen's gift was that which belonged to Michael le Fleming, which extended from Aldingham along the south-eastern side of the peninsula. Abbot Ewan, together with 12 monks from Tulketh, moved to Furness and chose to erect their monastery in the beautiful, secluded valley then known as Bekansgill,[1] at a point just about a mile from Dalton. The actual events which took place in this valley just over eight and a half centuries ago have not been recorded, but it is reasonably certain that the first buildings to be erected would be temporary structures for prayer, and to provide shelter while the monastery was being constructed. Just over four centuries later, at the time of the dissolution in 1537, the monastery was still expanding, and what had begun as a simple Benedictine abbey had by then become the second largest monastery in the kingdom, a glittering symbol of monastic industry and endeavour, and the source of Dalton's pride and prosperity.

The Importance of the Abbey in Dalton's History

Stephen's charter conferred almost regal power upon the abbot; a translation of part of it is given here:

8

In the name of the Father, and of the Son, and of the Holy Ghost, and in honour of
St. Mary, mother of our Lord, I, Stephen, Earl of Boulogne and Moreton, providing,
and seeking the help of God, for the safety of my own soul and that of my wife the
Countess Matilda, and for the soul of my lord and uncle Henry, King of England and
Duke of Normandy, and for the souls of all the faithful, as well for the living as for those
who have paid the debt of death, in the one thousand one hundred and twenty seventh
year from our Lord's Incarnation, the fifth Indiction and the seventeenth Epact, per-
ceiving every day that the span of life hastens to its close, that all the pomps of this
passing world, and the flowers and roses, the crowns and palms of flourishing kings,
emperors and dukes, and of all rich men, wither away, and that the materials of them
all alike are tending to one issue, and that all things are hastening with rapid course to
death, do render, and grant unto God and to Saint Mary of Furness, and to the abbot of
that place the whole of my forest of Furness, and Walney, and all the hunting rights
which belong to them, and Dalton, and all my Lordship in Furness, together with the
men and all things pertaining to it, namely in wood and in plain in land and in waters
and Ulverston and Roger Bristoald with his belongings and my fishery of Lancaster and
Warine the little with all his land and soc[2] and sac[3] tol[4] and theam[5] and infangentheof[6]
and everything that within Furness is contained except the land of Michael le Fleming . . .

This charter presented the abbot with about half the land in Low Furness and
also gave him the necessary authority to rule his subjects; but it is only part of
the picture. For most of the monastic era, the abbot's authority over his people
was exceeded only by that of the king, and the privileges he enjoyed were confirmed by no less than 12 successive monarchs and several Papal Bulls. Among
other privileges claimed by the abbot were:

(a) Exemption from the sheriff's turn. This guaranteed that the sheriff on his
    twice yearly tour of the shire was not permitted to enter the abbot's land,
    the abbot himself being responsible for the processes of justice thus
    excluded.
(b) Assize of bread and ale throughout Furness. The quality of bread and ale
    was often doubtful and caused concern. At this assize it was tested and
    presumably offenders were fined.
(c) Free chase through all Furness, and wreck of sea on the coast of Furness
    with the exception of Aldingham.
(d) He and his subjects were to be exempt from fines issued by county and
    wapentake courts.
(e) A free weekly market, fair and court of criminal jurisdiction in Dalton for
    the entire Liberty of Furness.

This is merely an indication of the sort of authority held by successive abbots,
and was in fact subject to slight change at various times in the monastic
period. On the whole it may be said that few abbeys, if any, could boast of
more royal protection than Furness Abbey; and of course the monastery became
very wealthy, not only because of its commercial activities, but also as a result
of many grants and donations of land and property by members of the nobility.
At the time of Henry II, the monastic possessions in Furness consisted of the
parish of Dalton, which at that time included the manors of Dalton, Plain Furness
and Hawkshead — a total area of 55,000 acres. In 1227 the over-lordship of the

manor of Aldingham was transferred from the Crown to the abbot, and the lord of this manor then had to render homage to the abbot together with an annual rent of £10. This meant that the abbot was now overlord of the whole of Low Furness. Combine this with the fact that he also owned a considerable portion of the land in High Furness, and had possessions in the Isle of Man, Ireland, Cumberland, Yorkshire and other parts of the country, and it will be immediately obvious that he was an exceedingly wealthy and influential person, and that the presence of the monastery so close to Dalton was a singularly important factor in the development of the town.

The Effect of the Monastery on the Population and Town

Customs of the Manor

The feudal conditions which existed in Furness immediately after the Conquest are now impossible to determine in detail, but following the foundation of the abbey it appears that the population of Furness was divided into three classes. The most honourable of these were the free homagers (socmen), who were exempt from villein service and were bound to the lord by homage only and the payment of rent. The next class down were the copyholders who possessed a court roll copy confirming their tenancy. For this they paid 4d.[7] and an annual rent, but were excused all other obligations except military service. The third class, to which most people belonged, were the customary tenants who were originally serfs, and thus banned from any tenure of property. Under the abbots they were granted the right to property, for which they paid rent and an admission fine and were bound in homage and other services to the abbot. Members of all these classes swore an oath of fealty to the abbot to be true to him against all men except the king.

Most of the manorial customs were concerned with tenure of property, the tenants' obligations to the lord and the settling of disputes and grievances. For example, it was stated that 'If any tenant should die not having an able son to serve the king, but a daughter, then she to have the tenement right; always provided that she shall not bring to the said tenement any person but such as the abbot shall be content with' and that 'if any tenant should find himself grieved at any time, he should abide by the judgement of the said abbot and steward, and xii men indifferently chosen within the said lordship; so that if the said tenant was not content, he should have another jury, paying 6s. 8d. If the latter jury found him guilty as the other jury had done; and if he would not thus do, he should be discharged and voided thence'.

On admittance to a tenement, each customary tenant had to pay a fine of 1d. (known as 'God's penny'), and an annual rent which varied in amount from one place to another. They also had to supply the monastery with certain provisions, such as wheat, barley, sheep, hens and geese; and they had to agree to provide a certain number of armed men, bowmen and billmen, horsed and harnessed or on foot, to defend the abbot's harbour at Piel, or for use against the traditional enemy, the Scots. Towards the end of the monastic era, the town of Dalton had to provide six armed men out of a total of 60 for the manor of Plain Furness. Other obligations on the part of some of the tenants included the supply of 160 cart loads of peat every year from Angerton Moss, and providing labour for the repair and maintenance of Biggar Dyke, a barrier erected on Walney Island to protect the farmlands against encroachment by the sea.

In return for these services, the tenants enjoyed certain privileges granted by the abbey. These included security of tenure in their property, their individual weekly share of about 600 gallons of single beer or ale which was distributed at the monastery, together with 30 dozen loaves of coarse wheat bread. They also received sufficient iron for the manufacture and repair of their ploughs and other utensils of husbandry, and timber for repairing their houses; they paid only one penny for their fine, and they were entitled to send their children to the monastery school. All things considered, it may be said that the benefits the tenants received from the abbey more or less equalled their customary obligation to the abbot.

Industry

In the early middle ages Furness consisted largely of swampland and primeval forest, besides the Domesday lands which had been neglected since the troubled period following the Conquest, and the energetic monks set about the daunting task of clearing this wasteland and rendering it fit for cultivation. Considerable tracts of land were cleared in this way and granges (farms) were established which were worked by an inferior kind of monk known as 'lay brethren' or 'converts'. The granges continued to be farmed in this way until about the end of the 14th century when they were rented out to tenant farmers. One undisputable benefit that the local farmers derived from the monastery was the fact that agriculture, which previously had been a primitive art in this area, was elevated to a more scientific basis as the monks instructed the locals in more refined methods of husbandry and the cultivation of crops. At this time, when a poor harvest could bring the population to the verge of starvation, any increase in efficiency could help to soften the blow, and was indeed a great benefit to the rather precarious existence of the medieval population.

There can be no doubt that under the guidance of successive abbots the economy of Low Furness was greatly improved, and in Furness, as elsewhere, mills were an essential ingredient of the agricultural economy. Some mills must have existed in the area before 1127, but the construction of more would have been necessitated by the influx of the monastic household and the population attracted by the abbey. Locally grown oats and grain had to be ground into flour at convenient sites within the orbit of the abbey; yet still the abbot was driven to importing 'victuals' from Ireland, sending his own ship for the purpose.

One of the assets of Bekansgill where the abbey was situated was the powerful stream flowing there, and by the 16th century at least five mills were powered by this stream between Orgrave and the sea. At the time of the dissolution of the monasteries in 1537, Furness Abbey owned all five mills and was receiving a total rent of £24 10s. a year for four which were let to John Barwyk. These were Little Myll, Orgrave Myll, Rowse and New Mylls. Of these there is only evidence that Orgrave Mill was built during the monastic government of Furness. According to the *Coucher Book*, Roger de Orgrave granted the abbot and convent an adequate site to be chosen by them for the construction of a mill in Orgrave.

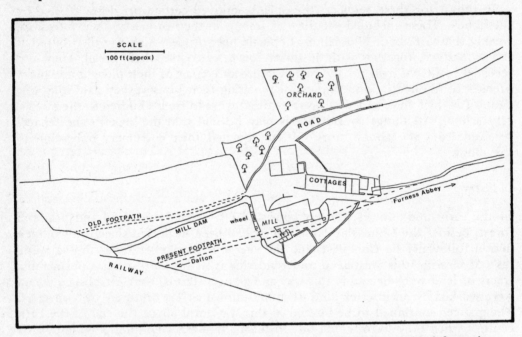

3. Site plan of Little Mill redrawn as accurately as possible from available information, showing the layout of the mill buildings with respect to the present footpath. Based on an old plan kindly provided by the Cumbria County Council Record Office, Barrow.

The fifth mill was situated within the grounds of the abbey itself and served to grind the corn consumed by the monks and the household. There was a clear distinction between the latter mill and the four rented by John Barwyk. Apart from the fact that they provided the abbot with a regular income in the form of rent, tenants of the manor were obliged to perform 'suit and soke' at these mills. This meant that they had to grind their corn there, repair the equipment when the need arose and keep the mill race clear of obstructions. They might have found that the 'mulcture' or payment for grinding their grain was less at other mills, but they were not permitted to have their corn ground anywhere else.

Another aspect of the monastic influence on the economy of Furness which must be mentioned is their development of the local deposits of iron-ore. This local ore is haematite, a greasy red oxide of iron, found mainly in pockets and fissures of the limestone areas of Furness and Cumberland, and to a lesser degree, South Wales and the Forest of Dean. The richest iron ore found in Britain, it contained in the best samples (found at Stainton) up to 70 per cent of metallic iron. This iron could be easily obtained by smelting with charcoal, a technique familiar to the ancients, and one with an undoubtedly long history in Furness, where charcoal yielding woodland abounded.

First surviving records date from the early 13th century, when the monks of Furness Abbey obtained rights to mine at Orgrave and Elliscales, and for the use of water for washing the mineral raised. The monks, far from being introspective contemplates, were pushing, practical men, wool magnates and landowners on a great scale, so it is not difficult to understand them embracing iron mining with equal vigour. These first mining documents are without date, but Orgrave is mentioned in 1235, Allinschales (Elliscales) in 1271, and Merton in 1396. These early deposits were discovered where the clay cover was thin or cut through by streams; the name 'Oregrave' (literally, 'ore diggings') occurs at Holme Green and also farther down Butts Beck. Supplies of charcoal for reducing the ore into iron came mainly from the forests of High Furness. Because charcoal, light and bulky, was required in great quantities, it was easier to take the ore to the woods, and the distinctive greasy red staining of the mineral still marks the line of the early trackways used. One such road runs from Oregrave Bank (Hoghouse Brow) through Tytup to Horrace, on Kirkby Moor.

In attempting to look back over almost 1,000 years, much inevitably remains obscure; but there can be no doubt that Furness Abbey stimulated the economy by bringing a degree of professionalism into agriculture, thus creating an increased demand for iron, mills, carpenters, masons, weavers, maltsters and many other supplementary trades.

Religion

Throughout the monastic era the religious members of the population were, of course, Catholic. The founding of the monastery in 1127 had little or no effect on their religious observance; they attended their parish church every Sunday, and looked upon the vicar as their spiritual leader. For the vicar, however, the founding of the monastery cannot have been a welcome event; indeed the whole history of monasticism in Furness appears to have been clouded with dissent and disagreement between abbey and church. For a more complete account of this unhappy relationship other sources (e.g. West, *Antiquities of Furness*) should be consulted; here, only a brief outline can be given.

Before and immediately after the establishment of the abbey, the parish of Dalton was very large, extending from the head of Windermere to Walney Island, including all the offshore islands. Obviously the vicar must have possessed considerable influence and authority, and this must have proved rather irksome to the abbot who was seeking complete control over the church locally. In the year 1219 he succeeded in his attempts to diminish the vicar's authority by detaching from the parish of Dalton the extensive chapelry of Hawkshead, where a new church was consecrated. This chapelry of Hawkshead was itself later subdivided by removing from it the chapelry of Colton and some other minor chapelries.

Quite naturally the vicar was opposed to this undermining of his authority and he appealed to the church authorities to reconsider the matter. The subdivision of the parish was halted pending an enquiry which finally decided in favour of the abbot, thereby severing once and for all the ancient bond between these parishioners and their mother church. This was the first step in the gradual decline of the parish of Dalton, setting a pattern which was to be repeated over and over again during the next 600 years. In May 1288 the abbot struck again. This time he succeeded in gaining control of the church, which was appropriated to the monastery by Walter de Grey, Archbishop of York. In this settlement the rights of William the vicar and his successors were protected by a reservation, ensuring them of a stipend of 40 marks per annum.

During the reign of Edward III, and under his auspices, an act was passed which decreed that '... an immediate parochial clergy were appointed, and vicarages endowed by such religious houses as were possessed of the parish tithes'. In effect, this meant that abbots of religious houses such as Furness Abbey were legally required to provide their stipends. Although for the clergy this was a step in the right direction, it still left them in a precarious position, for few of them would choose to argue too strongly with the man who had the power to evict them from their living.

Other attempts were made to improve the lot of the clergy, but only in a half-hearted sort of way. It was not until the reign of Henry IV that a statute was passed that brought a more realistic degree of independence to them. This stipulated 'that the vicar shall be a secular clerk, not a member of any religious house; that he shall be canonically instituted, inducted, and endowed with a sufficient stipend at the discretion of the ordinary, for the express purpose of celebrating divine service, for instructing the people, and keeping hospitality; and moreover, that he shall be a perpetual vicar, not removable at the pleasure of the appropriator'. This newly-found state of independence must have been welcomed by the local clergy; but it did not mean that the tension which had previously existed between them and the monastery evaporated overnight. In fact, it never completely disappeared. As long as the clergy suffered financially and through loss of authority, they felt they had a grievance; and, in the year 1423, another quarrel developed, this time over the payment of tithes. Both parties, the vicar of Dalton and the abbot, agreed to take their case to Henry Bowet, the archdeacon of Richmond, and to abide by his decision. This is an extract from the agreement:

This is the agreement, convention and composition, made between the religious men, Robert, abbot, and the convent, of the monastery of the blessed Virgin Mary, of Furness, in the archdeaconry of Richmond, and diocese of York, regularly possessing the parsonage or rectory of Dalton, with all its rights and appurtenances whatsoever, with the right of presenting to the vicarage of the church of Dalton, to their own proper uses canonically obtained, on the one part, and the discreet man, Richard Spoforth, perpetual vicar in the church of Dalton aforesaid ... concerning the right of receiving the greater and smaller tithes arising within the said parish of Dalton, under certain modes and forms described hereafter, and confirmed by the authority of the honourable Henry Bowet, archdeacon of Richmond, and ordinary, viz. That the abbot, for himself and his successors, shall have all manner of tithes, praedial, personal and mixt, great and small, oblations, obventions, mortuaries, fruit, emoluments and commodities whatsoever, arising within the said parish . . . the mansion-house of the said vicarage, together with the churchyard of the said church, with appurtenances, being always reserved to the said vicar and his successors. The mansion-house, with appurtenances, shall be repaired by the said vicar and his successors, perpetual vicars, reserving also the accustomed tithes of bread and ale in the town of Dalton, with candles that hereafter shall be offered in the church of Dalton at the feast of the purification of the blessed Virgin Mary, to the said vicar and his successors for ever. That the abbot and his successors, and convent, shall pay, or cause to be paid, for the time to come, yearly, for ever, by equal payments . . . the yearly pension of twenty-six marks of good and lawful money of England, in the aforesaid church of Dalton, at the feasts of the Nativity of our Lord, Easter, St John the Baptist, and St Michael the Archangel . . . In witness of all those things, the abbot aforesaid, and convent, set the common seal, and Richard his seal to these indentures. Done at the chapter-house of the abbot and convent aforesaid, October 10, 1423, an. 2 Hen. VI.

For the sake of brevity, the latter part of this agreement has been omitted. It contained a penalty clause wherein the abbot, in default of payment of the 26 marks, would be fined the sum of 40s. plus whatever the vicar claimed in damages. It also guaranteed the vicar 'personal and constant residence in the same church, as in law directed', and the right to perform all kinds of religious services.

Just how long and how faithfully this agreement was observed is not known; but the case serves to illustrate the state of dissension which existed between church and monastery, and is indicative of the fact that financial considerations (the vicar's stipend, right to tithes etc.) were a constant problem which was never really solved. The principal end result of this conflict is that the church at Dalton experienced so much erosion of its authority and independence that it became impoverished and its work suffered as a result.

Principal Effects on the Town

Before the monastic era Dalton was just another vill in Furness. It was probably larger than its neighbours Urswick and Ulverston, but even so its population was unlikely to have been more than 400.[8] Although no contemporary description exists, because the town was situated on a hillside plateau with definite topographical boundaries, we can be fairly safe in assuming that the whole town was contained approximately in the area now occupied by Market Place. Its physical dimensions therefore are unlikely to have exceeded 200 paces in any direction.

With the coming of the monks in 1127, a pattern of changes was established which resulted in Dalton becoming known and accepted as the capital of Furness. Perhaps the first major change was the establishment of the abbot's secular court in the town. It is not known exactly when this happened, but as Ewan d'Avranches had been granted jurisdiction in Stephen's charter, and he occupied the abbacy for at least seven years, then it could well have been within his term of office. In 1239, as a result of monastic initiative, the town was granted its royal charter — the first in Furness. By this charter Dalton was permitted to hold a weekly market and an annual fair on the eve, day and morrow of the Festival of All Saints (31 October–2 November). In 1246 a second royal grant was obtained for holding another three day fair in October at the Festival of St Edward the Confessor. This fair obviously replaced the first one because in 1291 the abbot claimed his fair by this charter only.

It is plain to see then that under the controlling influence of the monastery, the medieval township of Dalton quickly developed into a prosperous market town, and occupied a position of supremacy in Furness which was to last until an indeterminate point in time[9] some four or five hundred years later.

Local Government, Law and Order

The medieval system of local government and law enforcement was ingenious in that the people themselves were made ultimately responsible for their own behaviour. In Low Furness as elsewhere, the many hamlets with their town fields were known as *gravewicks*, and an eligible man (sometimes two men), was chosen by the Court Leet at Dalton from a list of names known as the *graveround*, to be head man of the village for a period of one year. He was assisted in his duties by one or more *painlookers* who were similarly appointed, and responsible for ensuring that the *pains* (penalties) and decisions of the court were properly enforced in their *gravewick*. The *grave* was responsible to the abbot via the steward or constable.

It was in the abbot's court at Dalton that legal matters affecting the entire Liberty of Furness were considered. Where this court was held, and when it first came to be held we do not know; but we cannot be far wrong if we place the date as early 12th century, and assume that the court was held in a building which formerly existed on the site where the castle stands today. The reasons for this assumption will become apparent later.

The Court Leet or 'View of Frankpledge' for the manors of Plain Furness and Dalton was held twice yearly – in May, on the Saturday following Ascension Day, and on 24 October.[10] In time, the October court became responsible for the appointments of two *painlookers,* two constables, two inspectors of weights and measures, two ale-tasters and one bellman. The Courts Baron, or Bierlaw Courts were held every three weeks for the recovery of debts under 40s. The record of an exchange of lands which took place in 1242, when Adam de Mulcaster exchanged a sheep pasture of 14,000 acres named Brotherelkeld, in Cumberland, for the monastic possession of Foss, is typical of the kind of business transacted in the court, much of which was concerned with the ownership or tenancy of property.

Obviously the court dealt with criminal matters too. On 7 November 1410, William Chaumpney of Kirkby Ireleth was tried for causing the death of Richard Dymer of 'Lees', by 'stabbing him with a dagger worth fourpence on May 12, 1410, at Dalton'. The victim died from his injuries on 8 June. There must have been some extenuating circumstances in this case, for it appears that the accused was pardoned. Later, in a case for recovery of debt heard in the court on

21 March 1413, John Del Schaghe (Shaw) of Furness complained that John Sanderson of Roose bought from him 20 ewes for 20s. on 17 October 1412, but he refused to pay. The verdict of the court on this case is not known.

It is a great pity that so many of the records of the court proceedings have been lost, for they would certainly make interesting reading today, and give us a more intimate knowledge of local people and the conditions in which they lived. In his book, *Barrow & District*, Barnes mentions the period immediately following the dissolution when the king's officers were clearing up some cases left undecided at the previous court, and quotes '... various persons fined for not keeping proper hedges in "Northscalefelde", for taking wood in "Sawreby" ... a dog known to be a "shepeworyer" is to be hanged, and scolds at Dalton are to be placed on the "cuckstool"'.

The question of the punishment meted out to criminals brought before the court is rather interesting. Certainly there was a prison in the town, where anyone convicted of a relatively minor offence could be confined, and nearby were the pillory and stocks. There was also a tumbril or ducking stool, situated according to one source[11] where Tudor Square is today; or, according to Mr. Stanley Fisher, former town clerk of Dalton, in that area close to where Station Road joins Market Street, and currently occupied by a doctor's surgery, the *Mason's Arms* and a decorator's shop. Until quite recently a farmhouse existed on the site where the surgery now stands, and in the property deeds it was referred to as Cuckstool Farm. Because this land is very lowlying, it is perfectly reasonable to assume that at one time there must have been a pond here; and, if this was the case, coupled with the fact that it is considerably closer to the old town, then this must be the preferred site for the location of the ducking stool. No matter where it was however, one thing is certain: centuries ago, at one or other of these two sites, many a garrulous old woman must have experienced the ignominy of a good drenching to the accompaniment of the jeers of her neighbours, for her scolding, vituperous tongue.

Regarding the more serious cases, crimes for which the law of the time demanded the death penalty, it is interesting to speculate on whether or not a gallows ever existed at Dalton. The only available evidence is both slender and contradictory, and can be used to both favour and deny the possibility. The following extract, from *Annales Furnesienses* by Beck, appears to suggest that the right to have a gallows in Dalton was one of the privileges already enjoyed by the abbot before being commanded to re-establish his claim to them:

In 1292 the abbot was called upon by a Quo Warranto to establish his claim to certain of the privileges and immunities he exercised in Furness. These were the sheriff's turn, amends of the assize of bread and ale, wreck of sea, infangentheof and free chace in Dalton, Kirkby, Ireleth, Pennington, Ulverston, Aldingham, Legh and Urswick, all in Furness: freedom from common fines and amercements of counties, and from suit of counties and wapentakes for himself and his men in the aforesaid places; holding a market and a fair, and having gallows in Dalton ... On the appearance of the abbot at Lancaster before the justices in eyre at the assizes held in Trinity term, he produced several charters to the court, and preferred his claim to the matters in question ... The jury by their verdict found that no sheriff had made a turn in those parts before the time of Henry III

> ... Also, that the abbot should not be free from common fines and amercements, and
> that he paid twenty pounds on that account in the very last year: but that as to the
> other matters, the abbot's claim was valid.

This last sentence is important, for one of the 'other matters' referred to was the abbot's privilege of having a gallows in Dalton. Yet from a document dated June 1293, we learn that the abbot had 'pillory and tumbril in Dalton only'. This, however, is rather vague, and can be interpreted in different ways; and it is the sole item of documentary evidence against there being a gallows in the town.

Perhaps the most impressive evidence concerning this matter however, is the fact that, just outside the town on the way towards Ulverston there exists an area previously known in an old property deed as Gallow's Land. This is situated where the new Catholic School now stands. On a tithe map of 1842 of this particular site, two fields are shown, one on each side of the road, and their names leave little room for doubt regarding their origin: field number A277 is referred to as Gallow's Bank, and field number A250 as Gallow Barrow Parrock. Add to this the fact that this locality conforms exactly to the type of situation frequently chosen for this purpose, i.e. just outside the town, on a hill and near to the main road, and one can not help but conclude that the evidence in favour of the existence of a gallows is considerable.

The Scottish Raids

Perhaps the most tragic time in the medieval history of Dalton was that 33 year period beginning in 1316. At this time the inhabitants of Furness must have been accustomed to hearing rumours of sporadic warfare near the Scottish border, for such disturbances were a constant feature of life in the northern counties and, indeed, were one reason why the parish of Dalton had to have a force of about 60 armed men constantly available. The members of this force wore armour or chain-mail and were armed with falchions (curved swords), bills (long handled spears with an axe blade and spike), bows, cross bows and spears, some were mounted and some on foot. To this day the tradition lives on in the town that the bowmen of Furness used to assemble on Goose Green before marching through the town to the archery butts (now Butts Beck) for practice with their bows and arrows.

We can imagine the alarm and consternation the inhabitants must have felt when in 1316 they heard the unwelcome news that a formidable army of Scottish warriors was advancing westward from Richmond Castle in Yorkshire, where they had devastated the countryside and successfully extorted a large sum of money from the noblemen of the district who had taken refuge in the castle. That these marauding Scots had a truly fearsome reputation cannot be doubted; everywhere they went they burned, plundered, raped and murdered with great abandon, and any resistance to their advance must have been impossible unless they could be opposed by equal numerical strength. The *Chronicle of Lanercost* tells us that after leaving Richmond Castle they marched west for 60 miles, 'laying waste everything as far as Furness, and burnt that district whither they had not come before, taking away with them all the goods of that district, with men and women as prisoners. Especially were they delighted with the abundance of iron which they found there . . .'. So it seems evident that in that year Dalton was burnt to the ground and many of its inhabitants taken prisoner or slaughtered. Whether or not our local defence force attempted any kind of resistance we do not know; but if they were wise they would have done as many of the townspeople must have done, and fled into the surrounding woods until the invaders had left.

It seems more than likely that at this time the abbot's courthouse and gaol were situated in a building near the centre of the town, probably where the castle is today. If this was the case it would certainly have been destroyed by the Scots, as would almost every other building which then existed in the town. After the Scots had departed, the task of rebuilding the courthouse must have been one of the abbot's first priorities, for law and order had to be restored, and it is quite likely that the new courthouse and gaol would have been built out of the ruins of the old one.

Only six years later in 1322 the inhabitants were faced with a repetition of these tragic events. This time the Scots were advancing from the north and were led by that redoubtable fighter Robert the Bruce. The abbot of Furness went to meet Robert and took him to the abbey where he was entertained and given a ransom payment so that the district should be spared. But it was not. Once again the Scots behaved with their accustomed barbarity, and Dalton, together with other parts of Furness, was mercilessly plundered. Richardson[12] presents a vivid picture of the brutality of these Scottish raids:

> It is difficult to imagine a more diabolical warfare than that waged by these barbarous soldiers from over the border. No rank or age and neither sex were spared; children were butchered before the faces of their parents, husbands in sight of their wives, and wives of their husbands; matrons and virgins of rank were carried away indiscriminately with other plunder; they were stripped naked, bound together with ropes and thongs, and thus goaded along with the points of swords and lances. In short, these brutal savages, to whom adultery and incest were familiar, after they were fatigued with acts of lust and violence, either retained the female captives as slaves in their own homes, or sold them like cattle, to other barbarians.

Some further indication of the disastrous effects of these raids on the lands and townships of Furness may be gleaned from the record of an Inquisition for the Wapentake of Lonsdale held in 1341, which tells us that 'The church of Dalton taxed of old at £8 is taxed anew at £2 . . . there lies in the same parish land uncultivated on account of the incursions of the Scots to the value of £3 13s. 4d.' Similar reductions in tax were granted to the churches of Ulverston, Urswick, Pennington and Aldingham, showing how thoroughly the Scots had ravaged Furness. The fact that almost 20 years had elapsed between the last raid and the holding of this Inquisition, yet there was still so much desolate land, clearly indicates that the population had not yet recovered numerically from the onslaught.

The Building of the Castle

After the last Scottish raiders had finally departed from our shores, heading across the Morecambe estuary for further plunder in Lancashire, the few pathetic survivors would be faced once again with the task of rebuilding their homes. Similarly the abbot would have had to consider rebuilding his courthouse and must have decided that this time, the new building would be a stronghold capable of withstanding any siege. So eventually, probably about 1340-50, Dalton's Castle or Pele Tower was built, at about the same time that similar structures were being erected in many other places in the north of England. It was rectangular in plan, with the east and west walls measuring 45 feet, and the other two walls 30 feet on the outside. At ground level the walls were about six feet thick. A spiral staircase situated within the west wall gave access to the two upper floors and the roof, and from the foot of the staircase a short flight of steps descended to the dungeon. The only entrance was via the doorway in the south wall.

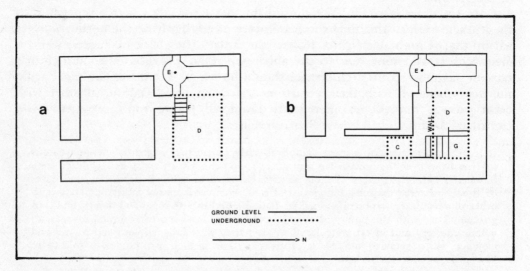

4. Ground level plan of the castle (a) as drawn by Close about 1805, (b) as surveyed by the Local History Society in 1978. 'D' is the dungeon and 'F' the steps leading to the spiral staircase 'E'. 'G' is the lower part of the present staircase. It is an interesting possibility that 'C' was the original dungeon and 'D' a store room.

These details have been derived from surviving evidence, both visual and documentary; but so much of the castle's early history remains obscure so that all we can do today is speculate on how it might have been in the 14th century. It is quite possible, for example, that originally it had a surrounding wall, and the building which we see today was the keep; but unless fresh information is unearthed, this must always remain nothing more than a possibility. The existence of a row of corbels projecting from the west wall, strongly suggests that at one time a building had been attached to this side of the castle. This must be regarded as being more than just a possibility, particularly after the threat of further military action had passed, because additional accommodation, perhaps in the form of stores, stables or living quarters for the gaoler, would have been an asset. A description of the castle in 1545 mentions 'the cost of repairing the said castle, *besides all the premises*' and this would appear to confirm the existence of other buildings actually attached to the castle.

This is about as far as we can go in meaningful speculation, but no matter how strong and impregnable this building may have been in the 14th century, it was certainly never called upon to fulfil its primary intended function — defence against further raids by the Scots, for, fortunately for the inhabitants of the town, they were never again called upon to face this particular horror. Instead, other terrors lay in store for them, against which the strongest castles in the land could offer no protection at all.

The Black Death

In 1348, people living in the coastal areas of southern England were alarmed at reports of an epidemic of plague currently raging in France and the Low Countries. Quarantine regulations were immediately imposed on all shipping, but to no avail, as the epidemic quickly established itself in the south and inevitably started to spread northwards, leaving in its wake a trail of half empty towns and villages. This particularly virulent epidemic, later known as the Black Death,[13] had established itself in the north of the country by 1349, and was ultimately responsible for the death of at least one quarter of the population of England. In his book *The Black Death*, Philip Ziegler informs us that Furness Abbey was severely stricken with this plague, and that many of the monks died. If this was the case, then there can be no doubt that Dalton was also affected, as all traffic to and from the abbey had to pass through the town.

It is unlikely that this would have been the first time that Furness had experienced plague, and memories or stories of earlier outbreaks would have warned the population what to expect. Part of the reason for their terror lay in their ignorance — they could not understand what was happening, and many strange theories were propounded ranging from the wrath of God, to a 'pestilential effluvia' carried by the wind. No-one gave a second thought to the black rat, constant and accepted companions in their homes and kitchens, and which were responsible for the spread of the disease through acting as host to the flea, which, when transferred to humans introduced the virus into the bloodstream. Although the presence of this particular epidemic in Dalton is not confirmed by any other documentary evidence, and despite the remoteness of the area, it seems unlikely that Furness could have escaped unscathed, and we can conclude with some justification that Dalton experienced death, despair and misery at the hands of this invisible enemy.

Let us conclude by trying to estimate from the slender evidence available, just what sort of effect this particularly disastrous period of our history had on the population of the town. To do this we must make a number of assumptions: firstly, that in 1316 the population was about 500. This is pure guesswork but cannot be far from the truth. Secondly, that each of the Scottish raids reduced the population by half, and the process of repopulation was so slow as to be negligible; and thirdly, that one person in four died as a result of the Black Death. Assuming that these conjectures are correct, then a simple calculation reveals that in 1349, the population of Dalton would have been just over 90. Although this figure may appear to be ridiculously low, and difficult to relate to Dalton's position as the market town of Furness, let us not forget that these disasters actually happened and the consequences must have been serious. We can only assume that the second half of the 14th century was considerably less tragic than the first, otherwise Furness would have been almost completely depopulated.

Chapter Three

TUDOR AND STUART DALTON

The Decline of Monasticism

THE EARLY monastic institutions so generously endowed and supported by the Norman kings and lords, were dedicated and sincere in the observance and practice of their religion. However, the inmates of these first monasteries did not know it, but theirs was an impossible dream; a curious situation in which the dream could never become reality, for the very act of trying to create and preserve this reality would inevitably bring about its destruction. From the moment they received the first gifts of property and land their fate was sealed, for this established the pattern of events which was ultimately to produce wealthy and powerful monasteries which, although superficially dedicated to the practice of religion, in reality were commercial enterprises on a vast scale. It may be thought that their wealth would make them secure, but as long as they owed allegiance to the king, they were vulnerable, and many a medieval monarch when contemplating his depleted coffers must secretly have regarded the wealth of the monasteries with envy.

Monastic wealth was not the only reason for their eventual demise however; this was merely a symptom of the malady which had infected monastic institutions throughout the country, and in Furness in particular. At the beginning of the 16th century, the penultimate abbot of the monastery was Alexander Bankes, a headstrong and domineering character who alienated gentry and tenants alike through his involvement in a constant string of petty squabbles, often resulting in expensive legal action. A full account of his iniquitous behaviour is beyond the scope of this book,[1] but this brief mention serves to indicate how the original monastic ideal had crumbled to a state of worldliness based almost entirely on possession and financial reward.

On 22 April 1509, Henry VIII became king of England, and in less than two months had married his brother's widow, Catherine of Aragon. The story of Henry's subsequent efforts to persuade the Pope to dissolve this marriage are a matter of national history and need not be described here, beyond remarking that the Pope's reluctance to concede to Henry's request eventually forced the king into taking matters into his own hands, and in 1531, Henry declared himself to be Supreme Head of the English Church. This was ratified by Parliament in 1534, when at the same time it declared that the king's marriage to Catherine was invalid.[2]

In 1532, after the death of Abbot Alexander Bankes and acting upon a recommendation from Thomas Cromwell (the second most powerful man in the country, who within the space of a few years had held the offices of Chancellor of the Exchequer, King's Secretary and Master of the Rolls, Vicar General, and Lord Privy Seal) the king for the first time took a personal interest in the abbacy of Furness and appointed Roger Pele to fill that position. From information supplied by Cromwell, Henry must have been well aware that Roger was as weak in character as his predecessor had been strong, and was not the sort of man to stand between him and the realisation of his main ambition, which by this time was clearly seen as the suppression of the monasteries and the severance of all links with the Church of Rome.

If the king needed any excuse to interfere in the affairs of the monasteries, it was readily provided by the inmates of the monasteries themselves as a result of their slide from their original high ideals, and in 1535 a commission of ecclesiastical lawyers was appointed to visit each monastery in turn and report on their condition. They visited Furness towards the end of that year, and on departing left a friar named Robert Legate with the Furness monks, ostensibly to read and preach to them, but in reality a spy for Cromwell. After the visitation, a series of injunction was issued to the religious houses concerned. This was a thinly disguised show of reform, the principal motive of which was to confirm the king as head of the Church in England, and to deny the Pope any authority at all in this country. New rules for the better observance of a truly religious life within the monasteries were also included, and a few short extracts are given below. (A full account is contained in West's *Antiquities of Furness*).

> Also, that they shall observe and fulfyl, by all the meanes that they best maye, the statutes of this realme, made, or to be made, for the extripacion and takyng awey of the usurpacion and pretended jurisdiction of the bishop of Rome within this realme, and for th'assertion and confirmacion th'auctorite, jurisdiction, and prerogative, of our most noble sovraigne lord the kyng and his successours . . . Also, that non of the brethren send any parte of his meate, or the levyings therof, to any person; but that ther be assigned an almner, which shall gether the levyngs, both of the convent and strayngers tables, after that the serventes of the house have had there convenyent refections, and distribute the same to poor people . . . and by no meanes let soche almes be gevern to valiaunt, myghtie, and ydell beggers and vagabonds, as commonly use to resorte abought soche places . . . to the great hynderannce and damage of the commyn weall . . . Also that no brother or monke of this house have any child or boye lyeng or pryvyly accompaynyng with him or otherwisse hauntyng unto hym, other then to help hym to masse.

Under these circumstances it was inevitable that the monks would become restless and apprehensive, for they wanted things to remain as they were and were reluctant to accept any change in their religion. Although their sentiments were apparently not shared by most of the population of Furness, as we shall see, many other people in the north of England strongly opposed the king's aims, and soon this factor, coupled with other grievances such as general shortage of food caused by poor harvests, increased rents and fines in manorial courts, led to such discontent that it finally erupted in open rebellion in October,

1536. This rebellion came to be popularly known as the Pilgrimage of Grace, and the rebel army itself as 'the Commons'.

In Furness, the atmosphere became tense. Rumour, subterfuge and suspicion flourished; and all the time Friar Legate was supplying Cromwell with reports of any treasonable talk or activities within the abbey walls. Roger Pele, the abbot, became alarmed for his own safety; so, accompanied by William Fitton, the deputy steward, he secretly sailed from Piel Island, to join the Earl of Derby who commanded the king's forces in Lancashire and Cheshire, at Lathom House. While there, he wrote to the monks of Furness Abbey 'bidding them be of good cheer, for he was sure on both sides, both for the king and the comens'.

During the abbot's absence, his deputy. Prior Brian Garner, supported by a monk named John Green, declared themselves in favour of the Commons, and commanded the abbey tenants to assemble horsed and harnessed at Dalton, on All Hallows Eve (31 October), to meet a Captain Gilpin of the Commons army. Failure to comply with this order was threatened with death or the pulling down of their houses – or so some of the tenants later testified. The tenants did meet, but they turned up unarmed and obviously not too enthusiastic about joining the Commons. Cromwell's informer, Friar Legate, was also present, and he, supported by the vicar of Dalton and Alexander Richardson, the Dalton bailiff, wished to open the meeting by reading a lesson of scriptures; but the rebellious monks refused to do this and urged the assembled company to join the Commons. They are reported as saying 'Now you must stick to it or else never, for if you sit down, both you and the Holy Church is undone, and if you lack company we will go with you and live and die with you, to defend your most godly pilgrimage'. All this was to no avail, for the tenants still refused to join them. The monks next called upon the vicar to come forward and be sworn to their cause; but he also refused, and the meeting ended with no-one joining the rebels.

So it seems there was little favour for the cause in Furness; yet, in other parts of the north there was considerable support, and the situation could have become serious had it not been for the fact that the leader of the insurrection, Robert Aske, while still commanding a powerful force, agreed to a truce and allowed himself to be fooled and consoled with vague promises that reforms would be made. In this way the revolt fizzled out, and those concerned in it, including Roger Pele, started returning to their homes.

The truce did not last long, however, for fresh trouble started brewing in parts of Cumberland and Westmorland. This was sparked off by disorganised groups of the insurgents who raided the tithe barns which were now held by the king's agents because there had been a poor harvest and a resulting shortage of grain. The trouble was easily quelled however, and the participants arrested. The local rebels from the Cartmel area were taken to Lancaster, where they were tried by the Earls of Derby and Sussex and Sir Anthony Fitzherbert. Four canons from the priory, together with 10 laymen, were escorted back to Cartmel across the sands, and on 10 and 11 March, 1537, they were hanged close to the priory, and in other parts of the parish.

The king now had the excuse he needed to blame the monks for these troubles, and the Abbot of Furness was a very worried man when he learned that, having finished their business in Lancaster, the two earls were going to visit his abbey to carry out an investigation. He warned the brethren to be extremely careful in what they said to them, and the possible dire consequences of any incautious word. The enquiry was duly carried out on 13 and 14 March, and at first it seemed that the abbot and the monastery were going to be spared, although two of the monks were arrested for a treasonable utterance and taken to Lancaster for trial. Soon afterwards, however, when the Royal Commissioners were at Whalley Abbey, they received a letter from the king informing them that, as the Abbot of Furness and some of his monks had been disloyal, another enquiry must be held. The abbot was summoned to appear before the Commissioners at Whalley and after a gruelling two-day examination, during which he confessed to nothing new, he was finally asked if he would surrender his monastery to the king. As the Abbot of Whalley had recently been hanged for his treasonable activities outside the monastery door, our poor abbot was not really in a position to refuse.

On 5 April 1537, a draft document was drawn up which, in effect stated that the abbot was willing to surrender the monastery to the king, and that he was doing this of his own free will, and no threats or other forms of persuasion were being used against him. In this way the scene was set for the inevitable and final act of surrender which was soon to take place in the beautifully ornate Chapter House at Furness Abbey, thus bringing to a close the 410 year existence of this once proud monastery.

The Dissolution and its Effects

Report from Parliament: 'The bill for Dissolution stuck long in the Lower House and could get no passage, when the King commanded the Commons to attend him in the forenoon in his gallery, where he let them wait until late in the afternoon and then coming out of his chamber, walking a turn or two amongst them, and looking angrily at them first on one side and then the other, at last: "I hear" he saith, "that my Bill will not pass; but it will pass or I will have some of your heads"'.

The Bill for the Dissolution of the Monasteries was indeed passed, and the first of the larger monasteries to fall into the king's hands was our Abbey of Furness. The Deed of Surrender and a translation of it can be seen on pages 28 and 29.

With the signing of this document, the fate of Furness Abbey, and also of Dalton and the surrounding area, was irrevocably sealed. Although the monks were permitted to remain on the premises temporarily, a start was soon made on the pulling down of the church. The destruction was continued by the Receiver Mr. Robert Southwell, who arrived on 23 June. After some slight initial difficulty with the monks, he finally sent them away with a payment of 40s. each (out of which they had to buy their secular clothes), to live as best they may. The servants and lay brethren were paid their outstanding wages and told to depart, as were 13 poor almsmen who were given one mark each and sent out to beg for a living. Eight widows who had been fed at the abbey kitchen were sent away with nothing at all, and other poor people who had depended on the monastery for subsistence were similarly treated. At the end of June there was a sale of all the abbey's livestock which attracted buyers from far and wide, but at which, according to Mr. Southwell, the poorer local farmers were favoured. All the abbey's possessions were disposed of in the same way.

The last Abbot of Furness, Roger Pele, on being evicted from the monastery was granted the rectory of Dalton, and he came to reside at the vicarage. He had barely established himself in his new home when he was informed by Cromwell that he would have to vacate the premises and find himself somewhere else to live, as one of the king's servants claimed a lease on the said premises. This elicited from Pele an urgent request to Cromwell to reconsider the matter and, as was the custom at that time, a bribe was offered as a further inducement. This is a copy of his letter to Cromwell:

My duete remembred unto youre good lordship I recommende me unto the same, Advertesyng yowe that I have receyved youre honorable lettres dated the XXXth day of Decembre last past to me addressed for oone lease of the personage of Dalton to be made unto John Bothe servant unto the Kynges highnes, wherein I most humbly beseche your good lordship, to be my good lorde, and to have me excused, and to consider, that I have nothinge elles for my hoole lyvyng, and except it to be for the avoydyng of youre highe displeasure I entende to be resident thereupone and never to make lease thereof, but according to the Kynges gracious lawes of this Realme, to expende the hoole profites thereof comyng amonge his pover Subjettes here which have great nede thereunto, And I have sent unto youre lordeship for a small token ffourty shillinges in golde, And that it may pleas your goodness that I may have your ffavorable lettres to be in quiett and peas wyth my said benefice wythout ffurther suete for the same to be made, I shall sende unto your lordship at Easter of such profites as shall growe due to me than, for a small reward after my power, foure poundes, as knoweth Almyghty Jhesu who ever have your good lordship in his blyssed vuycione. From fforneys the XJ day of January.

To the right honorable and his singular good lorde my lorde Cromwell lorde Pryvatt Sealle.

Your Oratour and beadman Roger Pele persone of Dalton

This unashamed piece of bribery appears to have had the desired effect, for Pele was still the vicar when he died in 1541. An inventory of his possessions, made soon after his death, seems to suggest that his life in Dalton had not been without its comforts. Part of it is reproduced here; for ease of reading, the prices of the various items are quoted in English, not the original Roman numerals.

In inventorie of all suche Goods and Catalls as were laitly Roger Peles, parson of Dalton-in-Furness, nowe discessed, made and indentyd the XXIIIIth day of May, in the yere of out Lord God MCCCCCXLI, before Sir Christofer Bolton, deayn of Furness, and prased by the holydome othes of Alexander Banks, Edward Pele, John Bolton and Thomas Walsheman. Inprimis, one bruying leade, price 5s. Item two bruying fatts, price 18d. Item one brasse possenett, price 2s. 4d. Item one panne, price 16d. Item eight doblers, price 4s. Item five dishes, price 20d. Item four sawcers, price 8d. Item one salt seller of tynne, one andyren, price 9d. Item two tryppetts (weights) price 12d. Item one yren speit, price 10d. Item raken crokes, price 6d. Item one parre of tongs, price 6d. Item one fyre shole, price 3d. Item one frying panne, price 12d. Item one cresshett (a lamp or

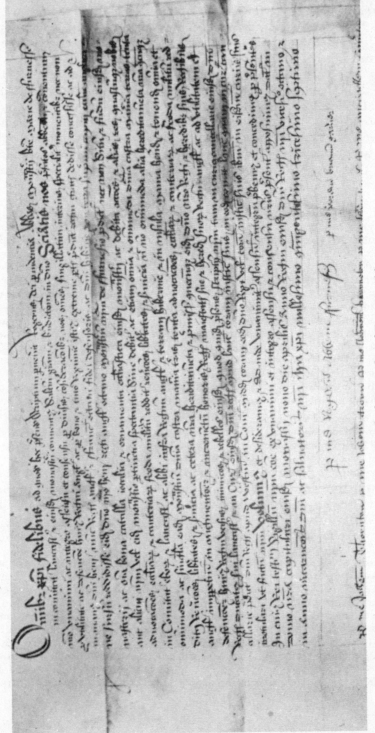

5. Deed of Surrender of Furness Abbey.

To all Christian people, to whom these presents shall come, I, Roger, by divine providence, abbot of the monastery of St Mary of Furness, in the county of Lancaster, and the convent of the said monastery, send greeting.

KNOW ye, that we the said abbot and convent, by our unanimous and full assent and consent, divers special considerations moving us interiorly thereto, as also for the use and defence of this kingdom, and for the good and safe government of these extreme parts of the said kingdom, have freely given, granted and surrendered up, unto the hands of the lord the king, that now is, Henry VIII by the grace of God, king of England, &c. our monastery of Furness aforesaid; as also the site and foundation of the same; and all goods and chattels, jewels and church ornaments, belonging to the said monastery; and all dues, actions, and other things whatsoever appertaining, belonging or due to us, or any of us, or to the said monastery; and also all manner of demesnes, castles, manors, lands, tenements, advowsons of churches and chantries, knights fees, rents, reversions, liberties and services; with all and all manner of our inheritances, in Yorkshire, Lancashire, or elsewhere, within the kingdom of England, in Ireland, or in the Isle of Man; to have and to hold all and singular the said monastery's demesnes, castles, manors, lands, tenements, advowsons of churches and chantries, with knights fees, reversions, liberties and services, and all other our hereditaments and premises whatsoever, to our said lord the king, and his heirs, kings of England for ever, in augmentation and increase of the honour of his royal majesty, and of his heirs, kings of England, and for the use and defence of this kingdom against its enemies and rebels. And moreover we will and desire, and unanimously give full consent, and grant by these presents, that this our present act may be inrolled as well in the court of the Chancery of the duchy of Lancaster, of our said lord the king, and in his own court held before his justices in the county of Lancaster, as in the court of Chancery of the said lord the king held at Westminster, in the county of Middlesex, before the said lord the king, and before his justices there.

In witness whereof we have, of our unanimous and full assent and consent, to these presents affixed our common seal. Given in our chapter-house of the said monastery, the ninth day of April, in the twenty-eighth year of our said lord the king, and in the year of our Lord and Saviour Jesus Christ, one thousand five hundred and thirty-seven.

By me ROGER, Abbot of Furness
By me BRIAND GARNER, Prior
and twenty-eight monks.

Translation of the Deed of Surrender of Furness Abbey.

lantern), price 6d. Item two stands, price 3d. Item one tablecloth of lynne, price 20d. Item one tablecloth of harden, price 4d. Item one tablecloth of dyaper, price 4d.

Effect on Agriculture

In 1535, a survey of the tenants' customary obligations to the abbot had been conducted by the king's commissioners. In this survey notice was taken of the supply of domestic provisions to the abbey, and at the dissolution the tenants were informed that the same provisions should now be paid to the king. Objecting to this proposal, the tenants presented a petition to the king's representatives at the abbey, in which they pointed out that in return for the provisions they supplied, they received from the abbey certain goods and benefits almost equalling in value the provisions they supplied. A compromise solution was agreed upon which committed the tenants to paying a rent in lieu of provisions, and the assessment was regulated in proportion to the quantity of provisions that each tenant had paid at the time of the survey.[3] This is one of the ways in which the tenants, old and new, acquired a greater degree of independence as a result of the dissolution; but, although the sale of abbey lands had encouraged new farmers to move into the district, the state of agriculture was precarious, and with the closure of the monastery the demand for grain crops and other provisions dropped immediately. The growing of grain was at first neglected, then completely forgotten as the farmers turned towards the more profitable business of breeding cattle. As a consequence of this, and other factors of a geographical nature, the Dalton market fell into a state of decline, and Ulverston, whose market charter (A.D. 1280) had not been made use of during the life of the monastery, became the new market town of Furness.

Effect on the Town

No contemporary documentary evidence relating to the effects of the dissolution on the town of Dalton is known to exist, so that all we can do today is to resort to guesswork, tempered with a high degree of probability from the few facts that are known. The principal point to be considered is the one which embraces all other minor aspects of the situation — the effect of the sudden closure of the monastery on the economy of the town and the prosperity of its inhabitants. As just about everyone in Dalton had depended directly or indirectly on the abbey for his subsistence, then the first effect must have been that quite suddenly many people found themselves without work, or at least that the demand for their services was diminished. In those days there was no social security as we know it today, with the inevitable result that many families would have been reduced to a state of poverty. There can be no doubt that the slump which followed the closure of the monastery contributed in no small way to the state of general apathy and hopelessness which pervaded the town for the next two and a half centuries; a marked contrast indeed to its former reputation as the capital and pride of Furness.

Perhaps a better indication of the town's size and prosperity at this time can be gleaned from an estimate of its size in terms of population, if we accept the broad concept that population trends over a period of time reflect similar changes in the prosperity of the town. To derive this sort of information from parish registers is not straightforward, as they only list baptisms, marriages and burials with no mention at all of the total population. But in Dalton we are fortunate that in 1631 George Postlethwaite the parish clerk informs us that the population was approximately 620, and this provides a vital link, for at this time the average annual birth-rate measured over a period of five consecutive years was 63. This means that there was one birth every 9.7 people. If we assume that this ratio remains reasonably constant, and that any other factors which may influence it tend to level out over a period of time, then by determining the average birth-rate over this same period of time, and using 9.7 as a multiplier, we can calculate the average population. Using this method, the following results were obtained for the period 1571–1630. (It should be noted that the Dalton registers date only from 1565).

		Dalton	Ulverston
1571–5	Average population	524	Insufficient data
1581–5		508	Insufficient data
1591–5		462	Missing
1601–5		466	514
1611–15		469	504
1621–5		435	Missing
1626–30		593	Missing

The figures for Urswick and Pennington for the period 1626–39 are 194 and 85 respectively.

At this point it must be stressed that these figures can only be approximate; nevertheless they do appear to be in the right order of magnitude, particularly when compared with the few figures it has been possible to produce for Ulverston, which by this time had definitely overtaken Dalton in size. To try to form any firm conclusions from these results would be presumptuous; but by extrapolation we can tentatively suggest that approximately five per cent of the population left the town very soon after the closure of the monastery, and thereafter there was a slight but steady decrease until 1590,[4] after which it remained reasonably constant for about thirty years until the sudden inexplicable increase in 1626.

An Era of Disasters

A glance at the diagram (page 32) clearly shows three periods of high mortality. This information was obtained from the parish registers — almost our only source of knowledge regarding the occurrence of natural misfortunes which afflicted Dalton so severely, culminating in the great plague of 1631–2. For a more complete understanding of the processes involved in analysing the information which is hidden away in the pages of the registers, we must first have a closer look at the documents.

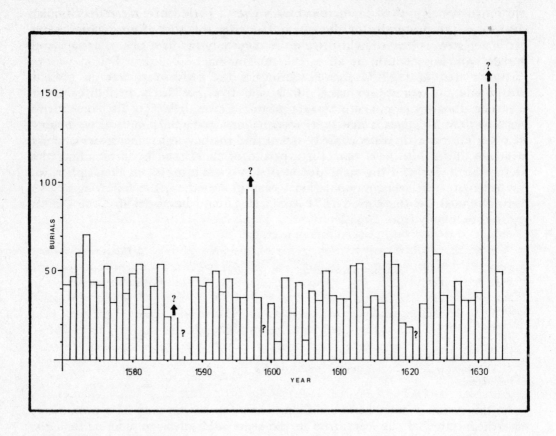

6. Number of burials per annum from 1565 to 1632. From the Dalton Parish Registers.

In 1538, Thomas Cromwell, the Vicar General, ordered that every parish in the country should keep a register of baptisms, weddings and burials. The main reason for this instruction was that the recording of this information would provide more reliable evidence of descent in legal proceedings, but it was also rumoured at the time that it was to provide a means of introducing new taxation, although this did not actually materialise for a very long time. As time passed, it became obvious that many of the earlier registers, which were all made of paper, were deteriorating quite rapidly. This was mainly because of the fact that at that time the paper being manufactured was of rather poor quality, and of course in many cases the documents were stored in damp cupboards or chests where they simply rotted away. There were also too many cases where the registers were completely lost or destroyed purely through negligence. In order to preserve the early information which still remained intact in the surviving registers, in 1597 the clergy were instructed to make parchment copies of all the old paper registers dating from the beginning of Elizabeth's reign. At the same time, they were instructed to make another copy of all past and future entries, to be deposited in the diocesan registry. These were known as Bishop's Transcripts. This means that today most of the registers dating from before 1597 are only copies of the originals. There are only a few of the actual paper registers still in existence.

Anyone consulting the parish registers today will notice that, in general, entries did not commence on 1 January, but on 25 March. In the Old Style calendar, this was New Year's Day. In some registers, however, the parish clerks seem to have had their own way of doing things, and annual entries commenced at other times. This is particularly noticeable in the Ulverston registers, where it seems that at different times the year began in March, April, May and even October. By Act of Parliament, the year 1752 commenced on the first day of January, thus introducing our present day (or New Style) calendar. it follows therefore that the previous year (1751) lasted only nine months. These peculiarities are important when determining population statistics, and dates should be adjusted to conform to the modern system.

The earliest Dalton register covers the period May 1565 to 1648, and contains 136 pages measuring 7 by 17 inches. The last 22 pages are damaged, and several others are now illegible due to being chemically treated by Henry Brierley (a former secretary of the Lancashire Parish Register Society) to render the faded writing more legible when he was transcribing this volume many years ago. In all probability the chemical he used was ammonium sulphide, and this has resulted in a darkening of the pages. Their contents are, however, preserved in his transcription. The entries were made two columns to a page — baptisms, weddings and burials — in this order, in monthly groups. (*See* page 34).

Although basically the parish registers are little more than lists of names and dates, all kinds of information is hidden away in their pages. This particularly applies to some of the later ones where other odd scraps of information (e.g. occupations) are sometimes included. To try to determine life expectancy, however, can be a time consuming and laborious task. This is because you can search through 50 or more years of entries following the baptism of a child, hoping to discover when he died, only to find that there is no further mention of that particular name. Further, because in small towns like Dalton and Ulverston certain family names were very common, and it was not unusual to find two or more people with exactly the same name. Because of these problems, and an acute shortage of time, an attempt to determine the average life expectancy of a Daltonian in the 16th century yielded only 10 cases, and this, of course, is not enough to obtain a reliable result. Nevertheless, from this rather inadequate study, it is perhaps surprising to relate that the average life expectancy in Dalton in the second half of the 16th century, was only 17 years. Part of the reason for this low figure, of course, is that the child mortality rate was much higher than it is today; even so, the longest surviving member of this group of 10 people was only 48 when he died.[5]

Although the case just quoted cannot really be regarded as being completely typical, it is an undeniable fact that life expectancy then was much lower than it is today. The reasons for this are not difficult to discover, being principally

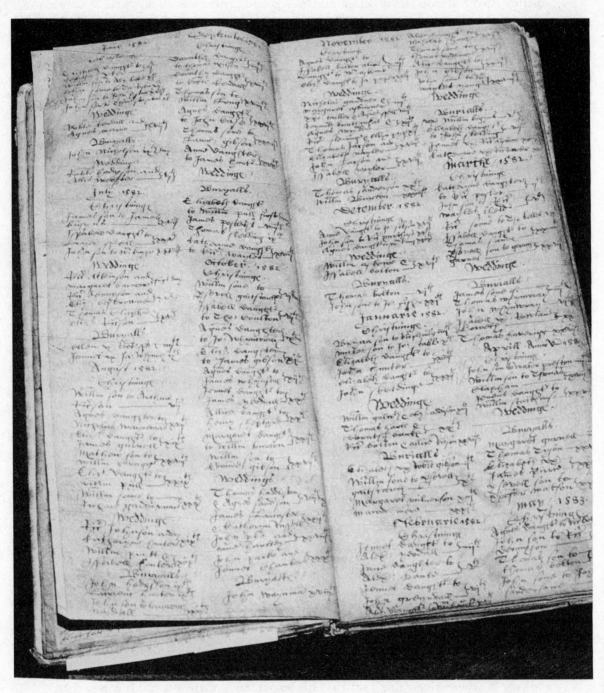

7. The first volume of the Dalton Parish Registers dating from 1565. By kind permission of the vicar, the Rev. Trevor Park, B.A., S.Th.

poor living conditions, and the deplorable state of medical knowledge at that time. To try to appreciate why the population was so vulnerable, and why an early death was almost to be expected, let us examine the background to this disastrous era and attempt to visualise what life was like in Dalton some 300–400 years ago.

Describing the town in 1631, the parish clerk wrote 'There is at a small distance from the sea and contiguous to the streams of a rivulet a town called Dalton which annually afforded sustenance to many poor people, to orphans, to blind children, and to those who were miserably lame . . .'. Although he does not specifically mention the mentally unbalanced, the old and infirm and those whose bodies had been wasted and ravaged by disease, they were all there, and constituted a considerable proportion of the population; potential and ready-made victims for pneumonia, tuberculosis, influenza and a host of other predatory diseases including the most dreaded of all — plague. The conditions in which these unfortunate people lived did nothing to improve their prospects of longevity, for there can be no doubt that the town at this time was still medieval; many of the houses were very ancient — cold, damp, draughty and infested with vermin; most inhospitable places by our standards, and almost tailor-made for encouraging the growth and spread of sickness and disease. There is some evidence to suggest that following the final plague epidemic in 1631, the appearance of the town was improved when many of the old buildings were pulled down and rebuilt.

One thing which immediately becomes obvious is that because of the appalling lack of knowledge about medical matters, disease and death were ever-present companions, and this situation must have been accepted as being quite normal by the whole of the population. There can have been no exceptions to this. The rich man in his castle could afford to pay for the best doctors available, but his chances of emerging fully cured from anything other than the most trivial of complaints, were little better than those of the beggar in the streets. The only slight advantage that the rich had over the poor, was that they were better fed, better clothed and lived in more comfortable conditions: a well-nourished body was more capable of resisting disease than the emaciated, wasted bodies of the poor, to whom a natural disaster such as a bad harvest, often meant that they were faced with starvation and possibly death. Having briefly established the background, let us consider how we can read between the lines of the parish registers in an attempt to discover what caused these periods of high mortality.

In his paper 'Disease or Famine? Mortality in Cumberland and Westmorland 1580–1640', Andrew B. Appleby of the California State University, San Diego, described a method of determining with a hopefully reasonable degree of accuracy, just what was responsible for these periods of high mortality, and the information given here has been obtained by applying this method to Furness, and particularly the Dalton parish registers. Anyone who is particularly interested in his technique, is recommended to read his paper, which can be obtained from public libraries. It is sufficient to say here that in almost every burial recorded in the parish registers, there is little or no indication of the age of the person concerned; and, as some diseases tend to affect certain age groups preferentially, any way of determining the age of the victim can help us guess the cause of death. Appleby used a method which, although unreliable, does at least render it possible to arrive at a child/adult type of classification.

Another important factor in attempting to identify epidemics is the time of year in which the majority of the deaths occur. It is quite obvious that many ailments can be attributed to the cold, wet days of winter, and there are others which thrive in the heat of summer; while others can occur at any time of the year. Nevertheless, when combined with known facts relating to weather, harvest failure etc., it is possible to reach some sort of tentative conclusion about the cause of these periods of high mortality. Typhus, sweating sickness, influenza, smallpox and dysentery should all be regarded as possibilities, as each took its toll of human lives in Renaissance England. Add to this the fact that during this period there were times of famine when the poorer people just did not get enough to eat, and, if they did not actually die of starvation, they became so weakened that they died anyway, from diseases which a stronger body would have shrugged off. It follows therefore that a combination of hunger and epidemic disease was a pretty lethal mixture, and it is likely that our ancestors in Furness had to face this grim situation on more than one occasion.

In the past, any period of high mortality shown in the registers has all too often been blamed on plague; but in many cases this conclusion is, perhaps incorrect. Take for example the incident at Ulverston in August 1551. During that month, 42 burials were recorded in the parish register, while for the rest of the year, an average of only four burials per month was recorded. In *Chronicles of the Town of Ulverston* (C. W. Bardsley and L. R. Ayre), this was reported as an outbreak of plague. Obviously something serious had happened; but was it in fact plague? Certainly the locals would have been able to recognise plague symptoms, and, if there is an ancient tradition in the town that there was an outbreak of plague in this year, then almost certainly it can be accepted as such. If, however, there is no such tradition (which is the case, as far as I have been able to discover), and no other evidence exists to prove that plague was responsible for this mortality, then we can say that the exceptionally long list of burials does not necessarily mean that plague was responsible. Plague was almost always associated with warm weather, so the month was right; but the pattern, although not impossible, was not typical of plague, which usually broke out in spring, increased in severity until the autumn, then died away during the winter months, perhaps reappearing the following spring. This cycle of events is dependent on the successful hibernation of the flea responsible for transmitting the disease to humans.

Could it be just coincidence that 1551 was the year of the last great epidemic of sweating sickness in England? This was a mysterious disease which struck with devastating speed, and has never been satisfactorily explained to this day. It was prevalent in the late 15th and early 16th centuries, during which time there were five distinct epidemics; the last one commenced at Shrewsbury on 15 April 1551, and rapidly spread all over England. If it was the sweating sickness which struck Ulverston at this time, then the incidence of deaths is in better agreement than for the plague, for in fact these 42 burials all took place over a period of only 11 days, from the 16th to the 27th inclusive. Then it was all over, just as abruptly as it came.

Moving forward some fifteen years to 1566-7, it seems that another crisis occurred in Dalton; this time it appeared to affect children more than adults. The following extracts from the burials listed in the Dalton register are typical of many:

Margaret Hunter	d[aughter of] Edmund	10 June 1567
Jane Hunter	d. Edmund	12 June 1567
Katheryne Hunter	d. Edmund	20 June 1567
John Woes	s[on of] Mathew	30 July 1567
Jenet Woes	d. Mathew	20 Aug. 1567
John Bolton	s. Roger	8 Sep. 1567
James Bolton	s. Roger	11 Sep. 1567

It is not difficult to imagine the grief experienced by Edmund Hunter and his wife on losing three daughters in the space of ten days. It is intriguing to contemplate the reason why they died. This was not a time of high mortality, so severe epidemics can be ruled out; but it appears that in 1566 and 1567, the death-rate among children was about three times higher than what can be considered normal. This fact has been derived from the registers by making the assumption that entries similar to the ones quoted above do in fact refer to children, even though it is always possible that they could be unmarried sons and daughters of almost any age. Assuming this, then in 1566 51 per cent of all burials were children. The following year child deaths accounted for an astonishing 65 per cent of the total. The average child mortality rate in the succeeding years was roughly 20 per cent; so it is quite clear that all was not well at this particular time.

We cannot blame the plague in this case for, if anything, there is some slight evidence that plague tended to spare the young and weak, and attack those with healthier and stronger constitutions. A more likely possibility may be dysentery, for this did attack children preferentially; but whether or not it was to blame in this case is anybody's guess. It would have been helpful if we could compare this with the situation in Ulverston, for then we would be able to determine whether this malady was purely the result of local conditions in Dalton, or if it was more widespread. Unfortunately this cannot be done because the Ulverston registers at this time only give a list of names, and there is no way of determining age.

1597 was a terrible year, not only in Furness, but also in the surrounding area. In this year, according to W. G. Hoskins, the harvest failed again, for the fourth year in succession; consequently food prices were high, and the poorer people, although perhaps not actually starving, would certainly have experienced long periods of hunger. This must inevitably mean that the population was in a weakened condition, and less able to resist disease.

Looking at the Ulverston and Dalton registers, it is quite obvious that the death-rate suddenly increased in the spring of this year, then the pattern changed. In Ulverston it remained generally high throughout the year, but in Dalton it fell to a normal level in the autumn, then shot up again in the winter. The problem is to decide whether starvation alone could have been responsible, or was there also some other external influence? If it was starvation, one would expect that after three years of rising food prices and increasing shortages, there would be a gradual increase in the death-rate over that period of time, and this is exactly what happened in Ulverston; the number of burials for each year from 1595 to 1599 being: 36, 64, 136, 72, 40.

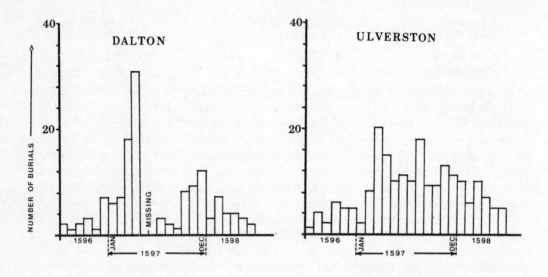

8. Comparison of monthly burials in Dalton and Ulverston in 1597.

In Dalton, however, things were different. The burial rate per annum immediately before and after 1597 was reasonably constant at about forty. So here we have two entirely different situations, which are really the wrong way round and different from what one would expect; for at this time, Ulverston's prosperity was increasing, whereas Dalton's decline was well under way. It is difficult to suggest an explanation for this.

The high incidence of deaths in both places in March and April does, however, look suspiciously like plague; and if we can believe the reports that plague principally attacked men and women in the prime of life, then this tends to confirm the idea that it could have been plague, for we can determine from the Dalton register that in March and April of 1597, there was no significant proportional increase in child deaths. There is yet more evidence indicating that 1597 was a plague year in Dalton. It comes from George Postlethwaite's account of the plague in 1631. 'Arthur Richardson said to many people, being impressed with trembling fear, "we shall be infected immediately with a violent plague, and I will forfeit my life upon the cross if this fiery pestilence rage not many months amongst us as we have seen before"'. From this it is quite clear that Arthur Richardson had already witnessed plague in Dalton, and, checking through the register we find that there was indeed an Arthur Richardson alive in 1597. To sum up, it would appear that both Dalton and Ulverston were stricken with plague in this year, and that other deaths, particularly in Ulverston, can be attributed to the effects of severe food shortage, possibly with an outbreak of typhus at the end of the year.

There was more trouble 26 years later. In Dalton there were 154 burials in 1623, and 59 in 1624. The average annual total for the four years before, and the four years after was 33 and 36 respectively. The number of burials in Pennington in the years 1622, 1623 and 1624, was 4, 25 and 8; and in Urswick for the same period, 15, 54 and 29. So in all these places, a similar pattern appears. (There are no figures available for Aldingham and Ulverston). It is clear then that the year 1623 was a bad one in Furness, and that the mortality carried over into 1624. It was not only Furness that was affected. Other parts of England experienced high mortality in this year, including almost every parish in the north of the country. The Cartmel registers show many deaths in 1623, as do almost all of those parishes in Cumberland and Westmorland that were investigated by Appleby. He concludes that because 1622 was a bad harvest year and caused rapid increases in food prices, the principal cause of the 1623 crisis was starvation. He supports this theory by quoting from the unusually explicit registers of the parish of Greystoke in Cumberland, where in March, 'a poore hungersterven beger child', and 'a poore hungerstarved begger boye', were buried. During the course of the year, there were other references to people dying from starvation. In almost every case in Furness (particularly in Dalton), the deaths reached a peak in the winter months; it is perhaps a reasonable assumption, that widespread famine caused such misery and hardship, and all that was necessary to send the death-rate soaring, was a particularly severe winter. This could well be exactly what happened in Furness in 1623.

The year 1631 was a plague year in Dalton and Biggar village in Walney. The parish register comments briefly, 'In this moneth of July 1631 did the plague begin in Dalton and Bigger; there died in Dalton of this sickness three hundred and three score and in Waney [sic] one hundred and twenty, it ceased about Easter followeinge'. Thanks to George Postlethwaite's account of this epidemic, we have an unusually clear picture of the strange and terrible events which took place in Dalton at this time. Postlethwaite, who was the parish clerk, entitled his account, *Lugubrious Lines on the destructive and violent Plague which raged in Dalton, and spread with rapid fury in the seventh year of the reign of King Charles the First and the year of our Lord 1631*. A more concise title could have been 'An account of the Plague in Dalton in 1631', and this illustrates the superfluity of words which is a feature of his account. The story that he tells is reproduced here almost in full translated from the original Latin.

There is at a small distance from the sea and contiguous to the streams of a rivulet a town called Dalton which annually afforded sustenance to many poor people, to orphans, to blind children, and to those who were miserably lame. Here various artificers, namely weavers, smiths, tailors, carpenters, shoemakers, tanners and respectable tradesmen, together with their assistants, obtained their livelihood and apparel. There also lived millers, malsters, glovers, vendors of ale and wine, mantuamakers, butchers, wool-spinners, many shepherds and husbandmen together with people of other occupations too tedious to notice. The Church of Christ grounded on a rock occupies an eminence near a small castle in the principal part of the town, from which the bells dispense a clear sound to a remote distance.

Six hundred and twelve inhabitants of different ages attended the church where the divine pastor who was the guardian of his Christian people diligently taught the word of God.

But now confide in what I say: the subject is not of small importance; therefore listen attentively to my artless strains. Although I, unhappy person could not describe the sorrowful events of the time which previously afflict my heart, were my powers of speech increased two hundred fold; yet, nevertheless I will begin; I do not intend to desist from my proposal.

In this town, sorrow with tears, lamentations and deep sighs began to prevail with the dire funerals of many inhabitants. A miserable, accursed, abandoned, vile fugitive named Lancaster with his wife came down from the superb city of London, bearing his own shafts of death enclosed amongst garments and precious jewels which were laid up as common report said, and the event verified in the death of the people, to destroy many of the living. These two persons brought in their baggage deadly poisons — a tartarean plague -- the sharp darts of a cruel death.

Arthur Richardson said to many people, being impressed with trembling fear, 'we shall be infected immediately with a violent plague, and I will forfeit my life upon the cross if this fiery pestilence rage not many months amongst us as we have seen before'. But yet notwithstanding this precaution we miserable people gave a kind of reception to those cruel enemies who were placed in the principal part of the town.

Presently the great power of the secret infection included in the garments burst out in a furious plague, the contagious fire of which blazed through the whole town and consumed the mortal curbs. And as the lopper of trees gives many wounds to the boughs with his hard axe and leaves the naked trunk so, alas, did the stranger Lancaster give severe wounds to us, then commenced physician, and administered poison.

Thus was the once cheerful town of Dalton oppressed with a grievous pestilence, and many inhabitants were its victims. Many with their families and household stock of provisions forsook their homes. The Rev. R. Tomlinson the minister also fled in fear, and left the holy threshholds of the church; and afterwards George Postlethwaite, the parish clerk, departed with hasty steps in the calm night. Every one hastened away protected by his faithful friend (the minister) and turned his back on the infected town. Many with straw and small leafy branches of trees constructed humble cabins in which were placed several infected persons, who might return to their own homes. Suddenly the plague raged with flaming fury and ultimate darkness closed many eyes. Then all the inhabitants began to quake with cold fear. They were astonished and, chilling horror raised their pendant hair, for the plague raged everywhere in the town and thence it was unlawful nay even impracticable to depart because the bridges and roads were attended by sentinels armed with clubs both day and night.

The pestilent Lancaster and his associate Noble, two wicked homicides who feared not death, nor regarded the Deity, committed the dead bodies to the grave with the falling of the dew.

In performing this office they placed the corpse upon a ladder, then proceeded hastily to the sepulchre, and there presumed to throw the body of a dear friend into the grave, as the lifeless trunk of a mariner is often cast into the sea; for the doors of the church were closed and the funeral bells were silent. Many people closed their own doors and sorrowfully wandered alone through the country over the fruitful plains. Boys durst not go with their mothers and fathers refused to associate with their children. Here the master was odious to the men-servants and the mistress to the maid-servants. Pale death gnawing their breasts, they drooped their heads and wandered in solitary places; odious and dangerous to all, the companions and friends avoided these miserable people like bloody monsters.

Sixty persons were sent to the sepulchre in eight days, nine of whom died in one night.

To many, the pestiferous Lancaster gave a kind of black medicine, the efficacy of which suddenly destroyed the memory and understanding of the sick person for the bloody plasma infuriates, thus the sick being delirious, beat out their brains against door posts and walls and perished ignominiously. Others he ordered to drink out of bloody cups, by which means they lost their senses and the whole use of reason. What demon could have invented anything more cruel than this?

9. The plague in Dalton in 1631. 'To marry, the pestiferous Lancaster gave a kind of black medicine . . .'.

At length the bells of the church began to sound, and the people performed the funeral rites with pious hymns and crowded together to place the body of a dear friend in the tomb, and as the furious whirl-winds in Autumn disturb the boughs of trees, and disperse the leaves upon the grass, so men fell by disease and filled the churchyard.

The neighbouring people gave many necessaries of life to the sorrowful townsmen and to those miserable persons enclosed in the gulf of death. The renowned John Preston Esq., worthy of eternal honour (whom may the celestial powers always preserve) took care to distribute milk, bread and money to the needy. This pious gentleman gave many presents to the little ones, and took care that the rapid infection of the plague should not advance, and spread abroad in other small towns.

After the violence of the plague had increased more grievously, it blazed with terrible fury in respectable houses. Then the prudent Justice of the Peace cast the pestiferous Lancaster and Noble his associate in the evil, into dark prison, where the depopulators of our country lived, as it were, in the gulf of death and received all the light they enjoyed through the chinks in the door. But they deserved punishment more grievous than this, they ought to have been cast into the rapid streams of the vast Phlegethon . . .

But this pestiferous, this false, this execrable barbarian, this abandoned, cruel outlaw Lancaster, presumed to administer dire infection to many, and his vile hands compounded poisons which suddenly penetrated the systems and broke the hearts of men. This craver of plunder and spoil for a long time drew the fickle vulgar into his false opinion by saying with open mouth (believe me) 'the disease is not to be feared'. Thus the people, blinded by false assurances, increased the plague by visiting their companions.

The consuming plague raged seven months in this town, with acute flames more fervent than the Sicilian Etna, and in this space of time, did cruel death devour three hundred and sixty inhabitants. I am witness to a great many burials.

After many sorrowful funerals and the destruction of the town, the people purified their houses with frankinsense, bitumen, myrrh, fictitious powder and sulphur, and, at the same time burnt their garments and infected bedding. All the inhabitants gave solemn assurance upon receiving the anniversary sacrament to surrender to the purifiers all goods retained in their houses without fraud or deceit, not to preserve anything stored in secrecy; because by clandestinely keeping infected garments, they might afterwards endanger the town. But yet, the wretched perjuror, Noble (a person false and belying the name) and his wife have privately concealed in a granary amongst heaps of corn, in beds, and other places which were opened in their apartments, rugs and many sheets, garments, gowns, shirts, webbs and several other articles privately collected in the time of the plague.

Lancaster and his wife do not now molest our walls, they lately departed (all glory be to God). But the pest bearer did not go off unrevenged by the hands of the women, who having vigilantly watched the gates and roads, assaulted him with stones which severely wounded his head, and then contended with crooked staffs. To those by whom the wounds were inflicted (but not without cause), the false, abandoned Lancaster pretended he was killed, and feigned not to inspire air, for the cunning rascal laid upon the ground as if he were dead, and thus the villain finally evaded the vengeance of the women and fled, which was pleasant and gave great joy to all.

This then was how George Postlethwaite witnessed this epidemic of plague in Dalton, and we should be eternally grateful to him for taking the trouble to write it down. One can't help thinking, however, that it would have been more informative if he had written it in English instead of Latin, for in all probability, some of the original meaning has been lost in the two translations involved - first from English into Latin, and then, years later by some other person, back into English.

It is, nevertheless, a rather strange and terrible story. That these cruel incidents actually took place in Dalton, is now almost unbelievable; but the fact that it was all caused by only one man, who could so easily have been turned away from the town, makes it even more dramatic. It appears that this man Lancaster because of his knowledge of 'medicines', and his apparent disregard for his own safety was in all probability a quack doctor. If this was the case, then he was just one of that great number of men who made a good living, selling their useless and objectionable medicines to a frightened and gullible public in plague-infested towns throughout the land, when the qualified doctors had given up in despair and fled into the countryside. Worse, of course, was the fact that because of his own immunity, such a person could easily be responsible for spreading the disease. His treatment of the sick, and presumably those who had not yet contracted the disease but feared for their own safety, was thoroughly barbaric, and was inspired solely by motives of personal gain. His only useful activity lay in the part he played in burying the dead. Yet, when it was all over, and he had been evicted from the town, perhaps some people felt a slight pang of remorse at the sight of his bruised and bloody body lying apparently lifeless in the road, after he had been attacked by a crowd of angry women, armed with sticks and stones.

The severity of this outbreak of plague must not be underestimated. Half the population died within the space of only a few months, and all trade and industry ceased. According to tradition, the dead were buried in a common grave at the east end of the churchyard. A mound of earth supposedly marking the site was levelled out in the 19th century, when the churchyard was being extended.

During the seven months that the plague raged in Dalton, the market was held in a reduced form just outside the town at what is known today as Anty Cross. It is possible that this rather strange name originated at this time, either as 'anti' or 'ante'; legends exist to satisfy both versions. One story which could conceivably account for the name relates that during the plague, the town was completely sealed-off and no-one was allowed to enter or leave it. Anti Cross was the nearest point of approach to the stricken town, and it was to this place that food and other kinds of provisions were brought and deposited, to be collected by the unfortunate inhabitants. Money offered in payment for these supplies would not be touched by the vendors until it had first been purified by immersion in a jar of vinegar which was situated there for this purpose. The basis of this story is that there existed some kind of barrier which could not be crossed in either direction, hence the name 'Anti-Cross'.

Another story also refers to the plague. This tells us that during the time of the visitation, the weekly market, which had always been held around the cross on Market Place, completely ceased to exist. To compensate for this, another market was held just outside the town at the nearest point of safety before the old market cross, and in this context 'Ante Cross' could mean 'before the cross'.

These stories are similar in detail. Both mention the plague and some kind of trading activity, and, as they comply with known facts concerning the town at this time, it can be safely assumed that each version could well contain some element of truth. Both these stories were derived from conversations with a number of elderly inhabitants of the town.

The Civil War

Only 12 years after the ravages of the plague had subsided, the country was divided by the turmoil and conflict of the Civil War. Dalton was once again to experience misery and suffering, this time at the hands of soldiers belonging to the Royalist and Parliamentarian armies in turn. Although Furness was not too deeply involved in the events of these troubled times compared with some other parts of the country we did, nevertheless, have our own 'battle'. By present-day standards, a skirmish such as this was would seem to be of little importance; but when one considers that, at this time, the population of the entire country was only about three million, and Dalton's population probably about five hundred, the sudden arrival on the scene of some two thousand five hundred armed men, obviously prepared to do battle, must have been the cause of great local concern.

For the following details of this affair, we are indebted to Mr. Thomas Park of Millwood, who was then the High Constable of Furness. The first hint of troubles to come was when on 11 May 1643, a Royalist army consisting of 1,000 horse and 500 foot, arrived at Conishead after crossing the sands from Lancaster. The local population offered no resistance, and the Royalists remained in Furness for three days, taking whatever they wanted in the way of plunder, and they finally departed after disarming the locals and being given the sum of £500.

Farther to the south, the Parliamentarians had been increasing in strength and soon their army advanced northwards and occupied almost the whole of Lancashire. The local Royalists, inspired by the success of the earlier Royalist raid on Furness, decided to raise a force of their own, with the intention of evicting the Parliamentarians. This force was under the command of Colonel William Huddleston of Millom Castle, who raised a regiment, and advanced into Furness across the Duddon. On arriving at Kirkby he combined with a small group of Furness Royalists and then moved on to Dalton where he established his headquarters. One of his first acts was to arrest as many of the leading Parliamentarians as he could, and they were then imprisoned in Dalton Castle. Unfortunately for Colonel Huddleston, his security arrangements must have been rather slack, for some of his prisoners managed to escape and succeeded in warning a Parliamentary force under Colonel Rigby, which was besieging Thurland Castle.

Colonel Rigby with some of his soldiers immediately left Thurland and headed for Furness arriving at Ulverston on 30 September, where they spent the night. The following morning (Sunday) his force left Ulverston and headed for Dalton, stopping en route at Swarthmoor where a prayer service was held for his troops. After the service he pressed on for Dalton, but after passing through Lindal found his path barred by Colonel Huddleston's troops who were positioned on

Lindal Close, blocking the road to Dalton. Colonel Rigby's force was smaller than Colonel Huddleston's and consisted of 500 foot soldiers, two drakes (cannons) and three troops of horse. The Royalists numbered about 1,600 and were mainly mounted. Despite their numerical advantage, however, the Royalists were neither as well armed or trained as Colonel Rigby's soldiers, a factor which was soon to prove disastrous for them.

The fight commenced with both sides lined up and shouting at one another while powder and shot were distributed to the musketeers. When all was ready for action, Colonel Rigby's force quickly took the initiative by making a determined charge which the Royalists were unable to withstand, and they were rapidly put to flight with their victorious opponents on their heels. Some were caught and killed by the pursuers and many others were drowned, caught by the incoming tide as they were crossing the Duddon estuary. Colonel Huddleston was captured with about four hundred of his men, six foot colours, one horse colour, two drums, an ammunition wagon drawn by eight oxen, as well as horses and arms. His work now done, Colonel Rigby left for Thurland Castle, after detailing a force consisting of one troop of horse and one company of foot to remain behind to quieten the countryside. This force quickly started plundering the area, and Dalton suffered considerably at their hands before they finally departed.

A second incident involving bloodshed commenced with the defeat of the Royalist commander, Prince Rupert, at Marston Moor on 2 July. After the battle he collected together the remnants of his force and eventually arrived at Hornby, near Lancaster. From here he despatched a force under the command of Sir John Maney into Furness. This force established their headquarters at Dalton.

Anchored at Piel Harbour was a small fleet of Parliamentary ships whose crews, inspired by earlier Royalist defeats, decided to drive Sir John Maney and his men out of the district. They joined up with some of the local inhabitants who had similar ambitions and, without any form of plan or strategy and in broad daylight, advanced boldly upon Dalton. Sir John and his troops were at a sermon when the alarm was raised and they took up their positions in a field about a mile from Dalton and quite near Furness Abbey. Sir Henry Slingsby, who had joined Sir John Maney at Dalton described the affair in his diary. 'The enemy had taken into a little town not above twice musket shot off from our horse. Their horse was not many and drawn behind the town their foot had taken, some into a pinfold that was walled with stone and stood in the middle of the town: the rest had lined the hedges on either side. Sir John draws his horse into three bodies, two he sends to beat off the foot, and himself charges directly forward into the town. After one shot given they quit the town and retreated to the rest of the foot in the field, those in the pinfold were taken and kill'd. Their horse had the advantage of a deep crossway, that our horse could not but with difficulty come at them; and seeing them not stick at any difficulty betakes them to their heels. They chase the foot to the very sides of the ships; their horse took by wayes as knowing well the country. There was taken besides killed, 200 foot which were sent to the Prince, and 17 sailors and some rich countrymen were kept at Dalton castle, whom the Prince had given for exchange and make their advantage by ransome or otherwise. We lost not any, only Sir John Preston had his horse killed, and it may seem that being down, some of the foot running by gave him a knock on the head, but some thought it was by falling upon a stone . . . his perfect sense and understanding recover'd not for half a year after'.

Local Government

Following the closure of Furness Abbey in 1537, the Lordship of Furness was retained by the Crown until 1540, when by Act of Parliament it was annexed to the Duchy of Lancaster. Some idea of the size of the Lordship or Liberty of Furness may be gained from the following list of manors contained within its boundaries: Plain Furness, Dalton, Bolton with Adgarley, Ulverston, Egton with Newland, Bardsea, Pennington, Kirkby, Broughton, Muchland with Torver, Lowick, Neville Hall, Dunnerdale, Blawith, Hawkshead, and Coniston. The ancient parish of Dalton consisted of the manors of Dalton and Plain Furness, together with some detached portions of the manor of Bolton with Adgarley and a number of ancient freehold estates. After the dissolution, for the purposes of the appointment of churchwardens, overseers of the poor, parish constables, surveyors of highways and the regulation of other parochial matters, the ancient parish was divided into four divisions or bierleys as follows:

Dalton Proper	(Central portion)	1,044 acres
Above Town	(Northern portion)	5,362 ,,
Yarlside	(Eastern portion)	4,010 ,,
Hawcoat	(South-West portion)	7,544 ,,
	Total:	17,960 ,,

The boundaries of Dalton Proper are shown on the map on facing page).

The authority which was created to control the administration of parochial affairs was known as the Four and Twenty, and consisted of six sidesmen from each of these divisions. The members of the Four and Twenty were self-electing. thereby guaranteeing the preservation of the autocratic nature of their society and the influence and authority which they came to possess. It need hardly be mentioned that the members of this group were principally wealthy farmers and landowners. The earliest record of the activities of the Four and Twenty in Dalton dates from 1573, when we learn from their record book that:

It is ordered by the said John Preston Esquire and the said XXIIIJ that all the howses and Lands w^{t}in the towne of Dalton and in the felde therof w^{h}h doe appteyn and belonge unto ye said prshe of Dalton shalbe from henceforthe letten unto these psons hereafter named for terme of their lyves Paying for their admission thereof two yeres rent for and in the name of their fyne PROVIDED always that if they or any of theym doe not from tyme to tyme repayre maynteyn and upholde the howses and the p^{r}mis-ses well and sufficientlye in all mann^r rep^{r}acone That thenit shallbe Lawfull for the XXIIJ for the tyme beinge to put eny suche pson forth of the said prmisses and they so put forth to be thearebye excluted of the same for ever.

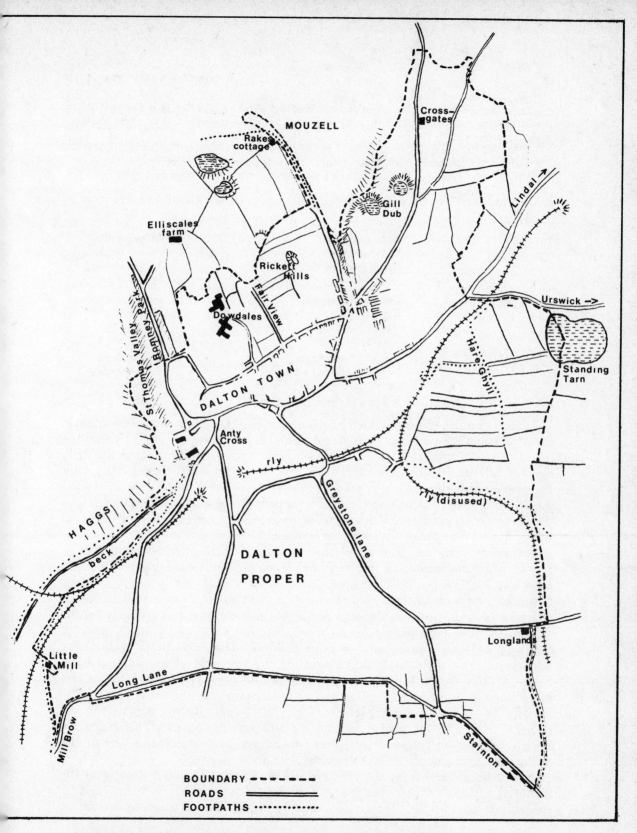

10. Division of Dalton Proper as derived from various tithe maps. Present-day features have been added to assist in location of boundary. (Note: western perimeter, i.e. Haggs area, difficult to identify precisely owing to indistinct marking on original map).

It is further ordered that when any tenn[t] of the p[r]misses shall Dye seised of anye the said howses and Lands That then his wife shall have and enjoye the third parte of the same Duringe her Widoweheade.

PROVIDED alwayes that it shalbe Lawfull at all tymes hereafter for the said XXIIIJ for the tyme beinge to Assign any poore impotent pson A Bedde rowme in the said prshe howses or Anye of theyme at their Discrecon upon neede shall require.

Some time later we have the following examples of weekly allowances paid by the 24:

1697	Widow Simpson	4d. per week
	Widow Dawson	8d. per week
	Wm. Taylor's wife	4d. per week
	James Mount	8d. per week
1703	Dorothy Ulverstone	8d. per week
	Kirby Child	10d. per week
	Widow Brigg	4d. per week
	Thompson's Lass	6d. per week
1704	Lame — Wm. Maison	4d. per week
	Infant — Askew Child	10d. per week
	Old & Lame — Beamon wife	6d. per week
	Old — Geo. Barker house rent	10d. per week

These examples give some idea of the activities of the Four and Twenty, but it is not a complete picture. Their fingers dipped into many pies and, within the broad framework of the law of the land they organised and regulated the daily lives of all the parishioners of Dalton. Above all however, they looked after themselves. One of their rules, made in 1697, stated 'that respect be had to the quality and birth of pensioners; and if a parishioner be an aged 4 & 20 man who should by God's hand or any other misfortune come to poverty, then he be served before any of that parish with a whole pension'.

For many years the poor people of the parish had no other recourse than to rely on the benevolence of the Four and Twenty for their subsistence. In 1626 however, Richard Gaitskill, who was the owner of land and property at New-biggin in Westmorland, conveyed the same in trust to John Preston of the Manor (Furness Abbey), who was directed to use the income from this property for the support of three poor people from Dalton, for advancing poor young women to marriage and the apprenticing of poor children. This was the first charitable bequest to the parish. Later he bequeathed the west end of his house at Bow-bridge, Dalton, for the lodging of three poor parishioners. This house later became known as the Bowbridge Hospitall and can be regarded as the town's first work-house. The site and remains were sold in 1804 to Mr. Robert Biggins for two guineas to add to his garden which was adjacent to the site. This charitable initiative was soon followed by others which were later combined to create the Billincote Charity which exists to this day.

It will be noticed from the first two of the examples quoted above that the manorial customs at this time are very similar to those which were enforced by the abbots of Furness. Tenure of property was still an important feature of everyday life, and continued to be the single most outstanding feature in the proceedings of the Courts Leet and Baron which were held in the castle. A document in the possession of Mr. Ernest Boddy of Dalton outlines the proceedings in these courts at a somewhat later date, quaintly, but unmistakably indicating their medieval origin. Part of it is given here:

LIBERTY OF FURNESS

Manors of Plain Furness and Dalton

'Oyez, Oyez, Oyez. All manner of persons who owe suit and service to this Court Leet and View of Frankpledge and to this Court Baron or Bierlaw Court of the Most Noble Walter Francis, Duke of Buccleuch and Queensberry now to be holden for the Liberty of Furness, for the Manors of Plain Furness and Dalton draw near and give your attendance'.

'Free Homagers of the Liberty of Furness answer to your names'. (Read same from beginning of Call Book).

'Tenants of the Manor of Plain Furness Answer to your names'. (Read the Call Book for Plain Furness. Mark those who answer).

'Tenants of the Manor of Dalton answer to your names'. (Read Dalton Call Book marking same as above).

Enter the names of the Jurors in the respective Verdict Papers and then make Proclamation once. 'Oyez, you good men that are returned to enquire for our Sovereign Lady the Queen and the Lord of the Liberty answer to your names'. (Read same from Verdict)

'Oyez, you good men that are returned to enquire for the Lord of the Manor of P. Furness answer to your names'. (Read same from verdict paper).

'Oyez, you good men that are returned to enquire for the Lord of the Manor of Dalton answer to your names'. (Read same from verdict paper).

Then swear the foreman. 'Mr. A. B. You as foreman of this Homage shall enquire and true presentment make of all such things as shall be given you in Charge and of all such other matters as shall come to your knowledge presentable at this Court. The Lord's Counsel your own and all your fellows' you shall well and truly keep secret and not disclose. You shall present no one out of Hatred or ill will, nor spare anyone out of love fear favour or affection or in hope of regard or gain, but in all things you shall present the Truth the whole truth and nothing but the truth according to the best of your knowledge and belief. So help you God'.

Towards the end of the monastic era, Dalton Castle, which housed the courtroom and gaol, had fallen into a state of disrepair. It seems evident that financial considerations had caused the later abbots to neglect the structure and pay proper attention to its condition, and in 1545, John Preston, deputy steward of the Liberty of Furness, and William Sandes, receiver, reported on its condition: 'There are three several chambers from the ground, one above another, all floors whereof have been made of timber. Now the said floors, as well as the Yiestes [joists], as the boards and planks, by reason that the castle has not been sufficiently thatched for a long time, are so rotten with water that has rained upon them, that few of the said Yiestes and none of the said boards and planks can be used again. The roof of the said Castle is also decayed for lack of thatch [lead] and like wise the window doers and the hinges and yren stayngers of the said windows are rotten, cankered and wasted away. The lime of the walls is washed

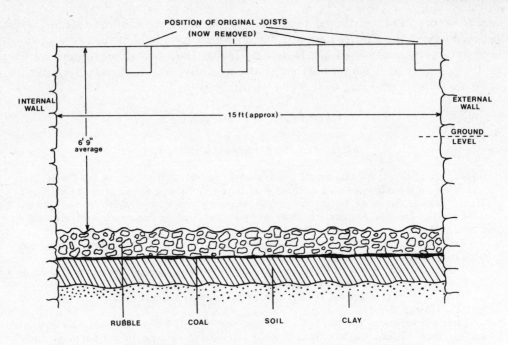

11. Section through the dungeon of Dalton castle, looking north.

out, so that the said walls are partly decayed at the corners and other places.
For the repairs thereof we estimate that six fothers of lead will be little enough
for the gutters and thatching of the said Castle, which lead may be taken of the
King's own lead lying at the Manor of Furness. Also sufficient timber must be
assigned within the King's woods for making the floors of the said chambers
and for the roof as shall be thought meet by the workmen thereof. We think that
half a ton of iron must be bought for the stayngers for the windows, hinges for
the doors, and spykyns or nayles for the flooring, which iron may be bought in
the country for about £4. We think that the cost of repairing the said Castle,
besides all the premises, will be £20 at the least'. The next year, Sandes was
directed to proceed with the immediate repair of the castle.

Markets and Fairs

Considering all the misfortunes that the town had experienced, and the fact
that by the end of the 17th century Ulverston had established itself as the
principal market town of Furness, it is perhaps surprising that the Dalton weekly
market survived at all. But the tradition was so strong that it did survive, though
in a reduced form. Unfortunately no description of the market at this time is
known, so further comment is not possible; but we do know that in October
of each year, Dalton's ancient market place became alive with the clamour and
bustle of the annual fair, an institution which was already several centuries old.

1. Evidence of earthworks at Elliscales (the farm is just off the picture to the left). The Dalton-Askam road is in the foreground.

2. Earthworks near Park Farm (just off the picture in the foreground). Possibly the site of a medieval farmstead.

3. (*above*) The castle and the market place, 1770, from a drawing by Thomas Hearne.
4. (*left*) Looking down the castle's spiral staircase.
5. (*below left*) The ancient doorway in the south wall of the castle.
6. (*below*) A Celtic stone head, found embedded in the wall of a house in Market Street, seen here on display in the castle museum.

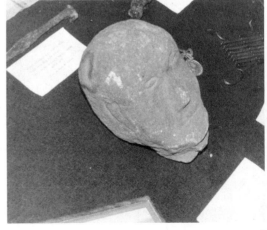

7. (*above*) Sixteenth-century Spanish cannon,
found off Piel Island, on display in the museum.
8. (*right*) Portrait of George Romney.
9. Romney's grave after restoration (1981).

10. Little Mill in winter: from an old drawing.

WHITE-HORSE INN,
DALTON,
(Lately Occupied by Mr. JOHN CARTMEL.)

JOHN GARDNER,

Having entered upon the above INN, respectfully acquaints the Nobility, Gentry, Travellers and the Public in general, that he has laid in a Stock of old Wines, Spirits, &c. and has made considerable alterations for their accommodation and comfort, and hopes from strict attention and civility to merit encouragement and support.

N. B. The above Inn is distant about one Mile from FURNESS ABBEY, and is in the direct road from ULVERSTON to that place.

August 5th. 1806.

G. Ashburner, Printer, Ulverston.

11. (*above*) & 12.   (*below*) Nineteenth-century handbills produced by Dalton tradesmen.

T. ROBINSON,

SURGEON, APOTHECARY, AND MAN-MIDWIFE;

Takes the liberty of informing the **Public** at large, that he has opened a shop in DALTON, and trusts by his Assiduity and Attention to those entrusted to his care, to merit a portion of Public patronage.

Dalton June 1st. 1807

Ashburner, Printer, Ulverston.

13. The pinfold for stray cattle at Goose Green.

14. Decaying remains of the workhouse cottages, built about 1825, at Goose Green. These cottages have since been rebuilt.

15. The old church from the cemetery; a photograph taken before 1884.

16. Skelgate in 1898.

17. St Margaret's Iron Church, Ulverston Road.

18. St Helen's Chapel in 1898: note the bricked-up east window.

19. The Holy Well, photographed about 1900 by Barrow Naturalists' Field Club.

20. Market Street from Gladstone Square, probably about 1910.

21. Tudor Square, c.1904.

22.   Market Street, c.1907-8.

23.   Market Street and the police station, 1910.

24. View from the churchyard, taken about 1912, showing the *George and Dragon* and a very young willow tree.
25. The same view in 1981.

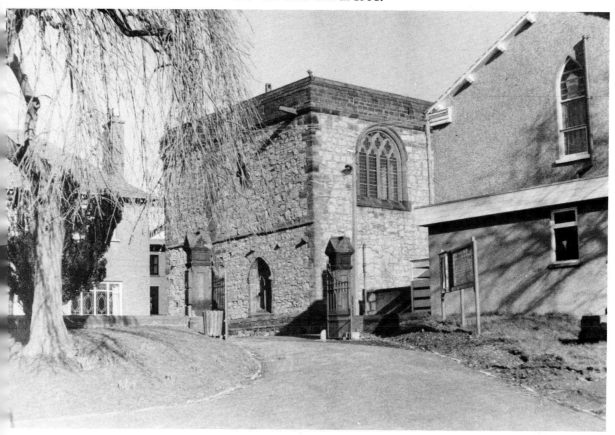

26. Dalton Casuals Football Club, c.1914.

27. Unveiling the cenotaph on Saturday, 25 November 1922.

28. View of the town taken from near the Station Bridge, before 1920.

29. A view of Dalton today, from the castle looking east.

30. Dalton ladies enjoying a tea party on the Weint corner probably c.1920.

31. Abbey Road, looking towards the foot of Mill Brow Hill, c.1920.

32. The Greenschool, c.192 Note Poaka Beck flowing by the roadside.

33. Dalton's first fire engine, c.1920.

34. The first motorised fire engine taking part in a street parade in the early 1930s.

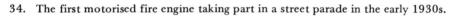

35. Miners at Nigel Pit, Roanhead, in the 1920s.

36. Station Bridge (date of photograph unknown).

37. One of the early buses.

38. View from the castle, looking north. The stone figure is the sole survivor of the four 14th-century originals.

39. Goose Green and the pinfold, seen from the cemetery.

40. Church Street. Note the columns at each side of the door of Bank House (centre), which originally supported the upper floor of the shambles or covered market.

This rather interesting description of the Dalton Fair is taken from *Furness and Cartmel Notes* by Henry Barber M.D.: 'The Feast of St. Edward is now held on the 13th of October, because that is the day according to the new style; but the fair is held ten days later — on the day of the festival of the old style, as is frequently the case. It is quite a common thing for the feast of the patron saint of a village church to be held ten days later than the proper date in the calendar, because the people follow the old style — so strong is the force of custom. The proclamation following is usually read by the crier of the Lord of the Manor, at the opening of the October Fair. It is a strange document, and from its quaint language, deserves attention. It is evidently the very same announcement that used to be made in ancient times, and was doubtless derived from His Grace the Duke of Buccleuch from the Duke of Albemarle, to whom and his heirs, all these rights, privileges and jurisdictions were granted by Charles II, A.D. 1662. There is such an unmistakable medieval tang about it and the wording smacks so much of the ancient times, that there can be no question as to its date and origin.

PROCLAMATION

Thomas Woodburne, Steward of the Most Noble Walter Francis, Duke of Buccleugh and Queensberry, Lord of the late Dissolved Monastery and Manor of Furness, and Liberty of the same, strictly chargeth and commandeth all manner of persons repairing to this fair, of what estate or degree soever he or they may be, that they and every one of them keep the Queen's Majesty's peace, every knight upon pain of Ten pounds every esquire and gentleman upon pain of Five pounds, and every other person upon pain of Forty Shillings; and that no person or persons have or bear any Habiliments of War, as jacks, steel coats, bills or battle-axes, but such as are appointed to attend upon the said Steward during this present fair. And that none do sell or buy any wares but by such yards and wands as are, or shall be delivered unto them by the bayliff of the town of Dalton. And the fair to last for three days, whereof this to be the second. And if any wrong be done or offered to any persons he or they may repair to the said Steward and have justice ministered unto them according to the law.

God save the Queen and the Lord of this Fair.

'It is very clear that persons resorting to Dalton Fair at one time were in the habit of misbehaving, getting up delightful rows and kicking up a "shindy" now and then, when the strong ale of the hostelries gave evidence of its potency by stirring up their combative propensities. In fact it was a sort of medieval Donnybrook, and men cracked crowns and slashed or punctured each other in proper fashion. The difficulties of such a situation will be at once appreciated when it is mentioned that Policeman "X", or "any other man" of the force of any letter or number, was not. The man in blue was unknown. The lieges of Dalton had to be otherwise controlled. The steward of the Lord of the Manor held his court in the grim chamber of the old Castle, attended by a force of halberdiers — "gentlemen in medieval smalls".

'The knight is seen on a prancing steed, caparisoned and "richly jewelled", the esquire upon a sorry nag, in the train of a gorgeous lady on an ambling palfrey borne, while the men at arms stand like statues (fiercely scowling from beneath their helmets) at the four corners of some gilded car, upon which sits in state, on a towering dais, the loveliest of womankind, surrounded by a group of resplendent beauties. Yes, that is the sort of character let loose upon the mob at Dalton Fair during any little disturbance or misunderstanding, in which clubs, swords, knives and quarterstaves were freely used. A metal hat like a porridge pot; a breast-plate like a waist coat of steel; and knickerbockers of substantial tin plate, jointed like scales on a hag worm's back, and rivetted so as to allow some degree of movement — such as would allow him to sit down, in fact. This individual carried a "most sayrious looking weepan" in the shape of a clothes prop with a bill-hook at the top. With this article he could, from the outside of a crowd, separate or grab hold of disturbers of the peace, or touch them up with the point on the end thereof . . .'.

From the same article, there now follows a copy of the Dalton Fair Tolls, dated 1716:

(1) For every beast, 2d. and for exchanged, 1d. of each party   ..   ..   ..   2d.
(2) For horses in like manner as for Beasts, Sheep 1d ..   ..   2d.
(3) For every load onions, potatoes, and wood vessels which come on their back   4d.
(4) For every parcel of ye same things not on horseback   ..   ..   2d.
(5) For every stand of pedlars who sell by the yard, Satturday being one of ye
       3 Proclamation Days this year   ..   ..   4d.
(6) And for every yard-wand to each of them ..   ..   1d.
(7) For every stand of hatters, pewterers etc. who break ground ..   ..   ..   4d.
(8) For leather sealing and searching, 4d. for every score of saleable bends,
       and 2d. for toll for each stand   ..   ..   6d.
(9) For every dicre of leather (i.e. 10 hides)   ..   ..   4d.

The Church

Following the death of Robert Pele in 1541, the name of his successor in the vicarage is not known. Some ten years later, in 1551, Roland Wright was appointed vicar and continued as such until 1558 when he was succeeded by Thomas Besbrowne (*see* Appendix One for a complete list of vicars). Although we have a reasonably complete list of vicars of the parish, at this particular time its history is vague, and we must move forward to the time of the Commonwealth for more details of the history of the church to emerge. In 1646, when episcopacy was abolished and the Prayer Book prohibited by parliament, Lancashire was divided into nine portions under the Presbyterian scheme. Dalton, together with Aldingham, Urswick, Ulverston, Hawkshead, Colton, Cartmel, Kirkby and Pennington, was in the ninth portion.

Throughout the country, the clergy was given the choice of accepting Presbyterianism or being evicted from their positions. The vicar of Dalton, Richard Tomlinson, accepted and became a Presbyterian minister. For the next 17 years until Mr. Anthony Turner became vicar, the parish church and vicarage were abandoned and neglected, although possibly some effort was made to preserve the church building by the utilisation of Parishing Rents collected by the church-wardens.

About the end of the year 1648, steps were taken by the Parliamentary authorities to increase the pay of ministers in poor livings, and in a document

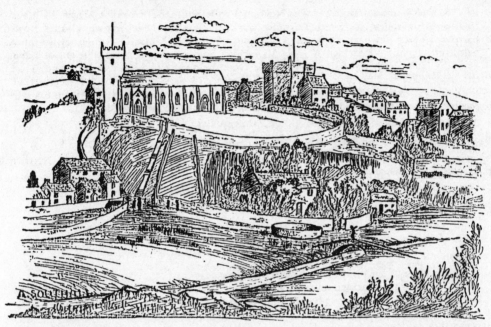

12. Early engraving of the town of Dalton from Mary Bank. Note the footpath from the churchyard to Goose Green, the pinfold, the workhouse and the school, and the apparently octagonal castle.

dated 3 January 1649, it was ordered that: '£50 yearly to be paid out of the profits of the Impropriate Rectory of Dalton in Furness, sequestered from John Preston, Esq., papist and delinquent, for the maintenance of Mr. Richard Tomlinson, Minister of Dalton, his present maintenance being but £17 6s. 8d. per annum.' In another document dated 26 March 1649 'Mr. Morris, Treasurer of sequestrations in Co. Lanc., [was] ordered to pay the petitioner, Richard Tomlinson, Minister of Dalton-in-Furness, all arrears of the £17 6s. 8d. his yearly stipend, and that Henry Porter and George Townson, farmers of Impropriation, suffer him to receive such tithes of the said Rectory as are already granted to him. Mr. Morris [was] also ordered to pay to the same all arrears of the £50 a year granted to him'.

It would appear from the following survey of church lands, which was published in 1649, that Mr. Tomlinson's stipend had not been paid for some time, and that he had been forced to rely on the charity of his parishioners for his livelihood:

And that the parish Church of Daulton within Fournace, & Co. of Lancaster Liberties (whose Long: is about 12 miles & Lat: 4 miles the Church seated almost in the middle) is a Viccaridge presentative by the Chancellor of the Duchy. The whole parish being impropriate to the heirs of Sir John Preston deceased a papist delinquent & the entire proffits received by those that have the benefit of his estate by Assignment of the Parliament. And that Daulton Parish doth contain the several Townships, Hamlets or Villages of the several distances etc. viz.: Daulton where the p. Church is seated, Irleth distant as aforesaid 3 miles Hacoat 2½ miles Ramside 5 miles Rouscoate 3 miles Pease-holmes &

new Towne 4 miles stanke 2 miles Newton 1 mile Southend 9½ miles Biggar 7½ miles Northscalle 4 miles Northend 3½ miles Cockam 2½ miles Oldebarrowe 4 miles Newbarrow 3 miles Newbarnes 2½ miles Salthouse 3 Lindell 1 Martin 2 miles And, there belongeth To the Viccaridge A little Viccaridge house & about ¼ of a Rood of Land And the Vicar hath no Tithes of Corn & Grain belonging to his Viccaridge And, That the said Vicar was in time past wont to receive £17 6s. 8d. paid by the Receiver of the Duchy Revenue but hath not been paid for about 7 years last past And the Vicar receives not any thing else but the benevolence of the people there residing . . .

The problem of the vicar's stipend and tithes was apparently never really resolved as, at the end of the 17th century there was still a good deal of confusion, as can be seen from the following remarks written by the vicar, Anthony Turner, and the churchwardens, on the subject of tithes and terriers. (A terrier is an inventory of church goods.) This was obviously written in reply to some previous correspondence:

May 17th 1968

Concerning Terriers

Dalton

The Answer of the minister and churchwardens.

(1) Wee have a vicaridge house built by the p'sent incumbent out of the Ruines of an old house, (their being before his p'sentac'on 17 yeares vacancy) Contayning three bayes of building— And a Litle old house Contayning two bayes of building, noe barnes, orchard or gardens.

(2) Wee have no gleab Lands belonging to our vicar save one Little pasture garth, adjoyning the Churchyard, being about a Rood of ground, no Chang(e) made.

(3) All the land in Dalton parish is tyth free or however payes noe tyth at p'sent to any p'son: (that is Corne or hay tyth) save the Lands belonging to Dalton— town, and the Lands that belong to the towns of Lindall and Marton: these 3 towns pay Corn tyth to the owners of the mannor of ffurnesse, formerly to the Abbott.

(4) To this wee give noe Answer in that tythes are nott paid to the Church.

(5) All the tythes of graine and sheaves of the 3 townes aforesaid are paid to the Impropriator And so is the tyth of wooll, Lambs, milk etc., throughout the wholl parish and easter oblac'ons, paid to the Impropriator or his assignes throughout the parish, the Vicar has only £17 6s. 8d. Sallary paid yearly out of the Rectory of Dalton by the Impropriator, and the Church yard (and Vicaridge garth and surplice fees,) as by an Instrum't of writing Dat: 2d Hen: 6th between the Abbott and the then Vicar: and Inroll'd or putt upon Record, that the Vicar shall have to himselfe tythe of bread and beare and candles through the said parish, butt is lost in tearm of tyme and alterac'ons of tymes and often vacancies— yet the p'sent Vicar knows nott what to make of it, nor how to begin to call for the same therefore humbly desires advice and assistance if it may be Reduced to the Antient Customs.

Anth. Turner

Vicar of Dalton

From the following letter written by the same vicar to his bishop, it is obvious that there is equal confusion over the use to which the rents collected from tenants of church houses should be put. 'The minister Adds and Saith that there are several houses in Dalton called Church houses or Parishing houses, which have tyme out of mind paid a Certain Rent to the Church amounting to £2 17s. 2d. or thereabouts. In the vacancy the Churchwardens Collected it And used it to the Repaire of the Church.— And since this Vicars coming have done the same— And would nott grant it to the Vicar-- though he hath several tymes Requested the same. The Vicar humbly prays my good Lord Bi'pp, his advis'r, whether he consider the said Rent to belong to the Vicar or the Repaire of the Church - And verily thinks the sidesmen and parishioners as well as himselfe would submitt and use the same as my Lord shall determine – for both stand Indifferent, and know nott well to whether use they p'ply belong– for the Cause is this they are called Church house(s) and ever have been, and pay no Rent to King nor Lord nor any assessment, only a Rent as afores'd to the Churchwardens neither is their any writing in any place found to express the use-- And the Vicar thinks that being given to the Church is to the ministry and converted to Church Repairs in tymes of vacancy, when the Churchwardens did alsoe Receive the said Sallary of £17 6s. 8d. from the house of mannor and therewith hired ministers for day, quarter or year as they could, - the benefit being soe Little nowe made for a p'sentac'on, till one Tomlinson who continued for a while and after Left it, and then 17 years vacant, and soe served by hirelings till Turner the p'sent Incumbent took and obtay'd p'sentac'on. In the tyme of Olliver the mannor and Rectory being under sequestration, And the sallary soe smale, And the Parish soe Large and Congregac'on so great: £50 per annum was added to the Sallary to a minister there out of the mannor or Rectory or both, butt att the Restorac'on taken away - The p'sent Vicar humbly desires a Considerac'on of these things'.

Education

It is fairly certain that there was a school of some sort in the town in the 16th century; but this does not necessarily imply the existence of a school building devoted only to this purpose, instead, it is quite likely that classes were held in the vestry of the church. It is known that in 1533 William Rede, who is believed to have been a former monk from the abbey, was dismissed from keeping school at Dalton because of the fact that he objected when 'a certain commissary and William Ashburner, one of the clergy at Dalton, had been persuading the people to pay Peter's Pence to the Papacy, in defiance of the Act forbidding this' and also for 'construing the Paraphrases of Erasmus to his scholars'. Unfortunately we know nothing more than this, but it seems evident that a school existed in Dalton at this time.

The first school building in Dalton of which we have any knowledge was founded by a gentleman called Thomas Boulton, a native of Dalton, who later went to live in London where he became an innkeeper. By his will dated 22 November, 1622, he left the sum of £220 for this purpose. To the Four and Twenty he also bequeathed the sum of 40s. to be used for the express purpose of purchasing a chest with three or four locks, for the feoffees (trustees) and their successors to use for storing their writings concerning the parish business, and this chest was to stand in the 'Quyer' of the parish church. He also stipulated that the trustees and their successors should keep a copy of that part of his will relating to the Free School, and that this should be read in the parish church every Easter Monday to perpetuate the conditions and terms of his will. In this, he stipulated that the sum of £20 was to be used as a contribution towards the cost of the building, and the remaining £200 used for the purchase of land which was to be rented out. The income from this source was to be paid as wages to the schoolmaster, except for a deduction of 20s. a year, which was to be used for the maintenance of the schoolhouse. Although today Thomas Boulton's will is no longer read out in the parish church on Easter Monday, it is commemorated on a plaque which may be seen on a wall inside the church.

It is an unfortunate fact that we have no knowledge of conditions in this school; details concerning the subjects taught, and references to the pupils themselves would have been fascinating to read about. We do know however that education for children of parishioners was provided free of charge, whereas children from outside the parish had to pay an entrance fee of 12d. The school itself was situated close to Goose Green at the foot of the cliff behind the vicarage garden, and initially had about twenty scholars. In all probability the first master of the Free School was the vicar, the Rev. William Bowett. The other known masters were:

Before	1680	George Postlethwaite
Approx.	1690	? Myers
Before	1705	William Lodge (Vicar)
Before	1707	Thomas Atkinson
Before	1758	Fr. Burton
Before	1764	William Thompson
16 August	1764	John Fleming
25 July	1767	Thomas Smith
28 July	1770	Martin Wilson Lamb
Before	1773	John Howson

Chapter Four

THE EMERGENCE OF THE MODERN TOWN

The development of the mining industry

ALTHOUGH IRON ORE had been mined in Furness for centuries, until the middle of the 19th century it was done on a comparatively small scale, and a general appraisal of the economy of the whole of Low Furness would unquestionably have defined it as being principally agricultural. Problems confronting the early iron industry resulted largely from an acute shortage of local charcoal for smelting, and primitive techniques and condition in the mines which made the industry very labour intensive and inefficient. Some smelting had always been done locally, but the industry received a substantial boost with the opening of furnaces at Backbarrow (1712), and later at Duddon Bridge and Newland. Because of the superior quality of the Furness ore, the merchants experienced little difficulty in finding markets and the demand increased accordingly. Eventually, ironworks were established at Barrow (1859), Askam (1865) and Ulverston (1874).

Even though there was a constant demand for the mineral in the early 19th century, there were still several problems facing the mine owners. Pumping equipment was almost unknown, with the result that only shallow mining could be contemplated, and then only in the dry season, because of flooding. Transport was also a problem. Before the opening of the Furness Railway in 1846, the ore had to be transported in horse-drawn carts, each of which held between a half and three-quarters of a ton, and the number needed was quite incredible. This created a bottleneck which effectively inhibited any rapid expansion of the industry until the coming of the railway opened the flood gates and paved the way for the boom period which was soon to follow.

According to J. D. Marshall,[1] in 1839 there were three main firms in the district: Harrison, Ainslie & Co. (Lindal Moor), the Ulverston Mining Company (Lindal Cote) and Thomas Fisher (Butts Beck, Whitriggs). By 1855, the number of mining companies in Furness had increased to eight. They were:

Harrison, Ainslie & Co.	Lindal Moor, Whitriggs, Gillbrow.
Schneider, Hannay & Co.	Park, Mouzell, Whitriggs, Old Hills, Newton.
C. S. Kennedy	Roanhead.
J. Rawlinson.	Crossgates, Carr Kettle, Rickett Hills.
H. Kennedy & Co.	Lindal Cote, Eure Pits.
Brodgen & Co.	Stainton, Adgarley, Bolton Heads.
J. & G. Fell	Stainton.
G. B. Ashburner	Elliscales.

It is clear from this that by the middle of the century Dalton was surrounded by mine workings, and it is not surprising that its population tripled between 1841 and 1871, thus creating a new Dalton — the principal mining town of Furness.

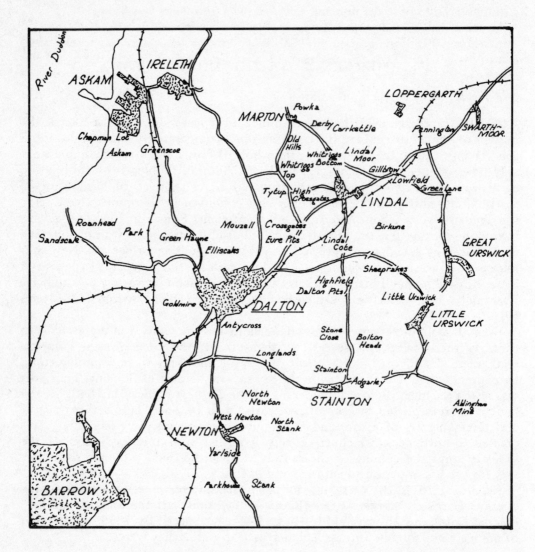

13. Mining areas around Dalton. 19th–early 20th century.

The picture, however, was not static. Prospecting for new orebodies was continuous and new pits were opened as older ones closed down either through being worked-out or because of flooding. Only the largest pits had surface installations with any degree of permanence, thus it was not uncommon for miners to have to walk several miles from their homes to their place of work, as new pits were developed. Machinery was slowly introduced, particularly to the larger mines; but in many places ancient methods were still being employed. Sometimes a hand windlass sufficed, and often a horse walking in circles around a drum served to raise the mineral. Life was hard for miners and horses.

Mention has already been made of the fact that working conditions in the mines around Dalton were primitive, particularly in the early part of the 19th century when industrial safety matters were left largely in the hands of the mine owners. What legislation there was to protect the workforce was cumbersome and easily evaded by the employers, with the result that working conditions were often extremely hazardous. The following extracts from the diary of William Fisher, a Furness yeoman farmer gives an eloquent indication of life and death in the local mines.

March 1827	Thomas Sowerbuts killd at the Iron Ore Pits by the roof of the pit falling in.
Nov. 25, 1828	James Benson of Ireleth & John Brockbank of Dalton wear sufacated by the foul air at Crossgates Iron Ore pit there was two others in at the same time which escaped with difficulty by accending the shaft in the bucket both the unfortunate men have left widdows and small famileys to bewail there loss.
May 26, 1838	Two men named Anthony Wall and David Parkinson was suffocated at Stainton Iron Ore works by the cabbin taking fire and the smook decending down the shaft Wall has left a widow and seven Childer Parkinson has left a widow but no family.
Mar. 5, 1840	as William Thompson and James Kendal of Martin were sitting upon a plank at Lindal Iron Ore works the ground fell in and buried them about 3 yards deep the[y] were dug out immediately but quite dead several others wear upon the same place but all escaped unhurt.
Oct. 11, 1841	Thos. Lowrey of Dalton Killd at Buttsbeck Iron Ore works by aporshon of the roof comming down upon him two or three more had a narrow escape it was two days and a night before the[y] got him out.
Nov. 28, 1848	a boy lost his Life at Orgrave Mill Iron works by his close getting entangled in the Masenery he was drown in and Killd Instantinely aged 15 years.
Jul. 25, 1850	Thos Dixon of Dalton met with his death under the following sircumstances he was carting Iron Ore from Eliscales to wate Flat and in desinding the steep hill at St. Hellins the stays of one of the horses broke and the animal took fright and diseased in is attempt to stop it was thrown backward on the road and the Cart passed over him nearly severing his hed from his body and killing him instantly he was 51 years of age.
Feb. 18, 1854	five men blocked up in a Iron Ore Pit at Park near Dalton by the bursting in of a pond of Water three was drowned and two taken out alive but one died the fowling day.

By the end of the 19th century it is clear that the once peaceful countryside around the town was spoiled and cluttered with unsightly mineworkings, and an intricate web of mineral railway lines for transporting the ore to the Furness Railway depots. It was not only the countryside which was affected, but the character of the town itself which was changed almost beyond recognition by the upheaval of this last half century.

The Effects of the Mining Industry on Town Size and the Local Economy

In discussing the effects that the mining industry had on the town, for purposes of comparison we should first look at the way things were before the mines opened. At the beginning of the 19th century Dalton was a small agricultural town, consisting of a single street which extended from Market Place to Tudor Square (or Bally Green as it was then known). From the Returns of the Overseers of the Poor, taken on 27 May 1811, we learn that the population of the parish was 2,074, and that of this total 329 families were chiefly employed in agriculture, and that the average number of persons in each family was five. If we make the modest assumption that two members of each family were employed, then 31 per cent of the total population were employed on the land. By 1834, 28 per cent of the population were employed in agriculture, and by 1841, at the time of the census, the figure had fallen to about 21 per cent. At first glance, these figures could be interpreted as showing a decline in agriculture over this 30 year period. This was not the case however because the population was continually increasing, and the actual number of people engaged in agriculture remained reasonably constant at about 700.

Perhaps some slight indication of the local importance of agriculture can be gleaned from the fact that at this time Dalton was the centre for the annual hiring of farm-hands for the whole of Furness; a practice which, because it was carried out on Sundays, and also because it was responsible for much drunkenness and disorderly behaviour, caused a storm of indignant protest from many of the townspeople. Writing about this, William Close commented: 'Because all the wheat in the area is ripe at about the same time, great numbers of hands are required for reaping, so the wages of these labourers who come from all parts and are generally hired at Dalton are sometimes extraordinary high. Generally in the busiest week, the farmer is obliged to give from five shillings to seven shillings a day, with meals and a plentiful supply of drink'. It appears that the purpose of this Sunday hiring was to enable the servants to start work with their new masters on the Monday morning; but it did not always work out this way, as many of the hired hands had still not recovered sufficiently from their intensive drinking bout to be capable of work for some time.

Another industry which flourished for many years in the town was the manufacture of malt, and on Horatio Merryweather's map of Dalton as it was in 1825 (*see* p. 66), there are two malt kilns shown — one at the junction of what is now Station Road and Market Street where Barclay's Bank stands, and the other in Market Street almost opposite the *Wellington Hotel*. According to Parson and White's *Directory* of 1829, there were at this time seven maltsters in the town. Some of these were probably only small concerns, as at least two of them combined malting with some other trade — one was also a butcher, and the other a coal merchant. By the end of the 19th century, all the maltings in the town had closed down. The following article taken from the *Barrow News* for Saturday, 11 January 1930 presents us with an interesting insight into the way at least one of the malt kilns in the town operated: '. . . malt kiln on the corner where the bank is now, and where the boys used to go to tread the malt, receiving in payment a drink of the brew. The grain was allowed to sprout a little and was then dried and spread on the floor. A line of boys would go on to it barefooted and tread in file up and down to break off the growth, the remaining grain being boiled and brewed. Dalton, once of local fame for many malt kilns and breweries, now possesses not one'.

The graph (below) shows the rapid increase in population that the parish of Dalton experienced after about 1840. From 1840 to approximately 1860, this

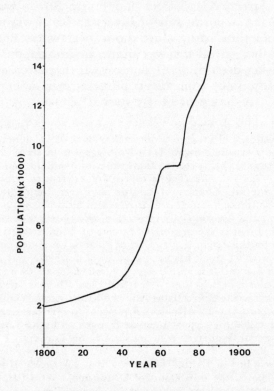

14. Population of the parish of Dalton. 19th century.

increase was largely due to a sudden influx of miners who had come to Dalton in search of work; but not entirely so, because at this time Barrow was included in the parish, and as a growing industrial town was itself attracting population. In 1871, the borough of Barrow was detached from the parish of Dalton; but it will be noticed that the population still continued to soar, and this is all the more remarkable because the parish was now less than half its former size. It can be truly said that the second half of the 19th century saw the birth of Dalton as a mining town, evidence of which can be seen today in the rows of terraced houses hastily built in this period as accommodation for the miners.

This flurry of building in the latter part of the 19th century created Dalton almost as we know it today, with rows of houses standing where once there had been meadows, fields and pastures. Cleator Street, for example, was built on a croft belonging to Miss Cleator, and which stretched in a long, narrow strip from Market Street to the lane which is now Chapel Street. Farther down the hillside towards the centre of the town was Dalton Meadow, also situated between Market Street and the lower end of this same lane, which incorporated land now occupied by Wellington Street, Nelson Street, and up to where Fell Croft now stands. This latter was built on a croft owned by a Mr. Andrew Atkinson. The area around Queen Street, King Street and Prince Street was known as Yarl Well Fields, and on the opposite side of Ulverston Road was a large open area, terminating at the old tithe barn, which stood near where Beckside Lane joins Ulverston Road, and this general area was known as Crooklands.

The earliest surviving description of the town is that given by Master William Fell, who described a journey from Ulverston to Furness Abbey which he undertook in the year 1777, at the age of 11. We start at Lindal:

> The Road to Whitehaven is through the Town of Lindale, but to Dalton is by a Smithy, and by some white Gates, and a rugged Stone in the Shape of a Column, which stands up in a Field, and makes a very odd Sight. Then Whitriggs is to be seen, which maketh a far more different Appearance, being red; so that white on one Side, and red on the other pleaseth thine Sight. The next Building is called Tythe Barn, to which, I understand, every Farmer about the said Country of Lindale pays every tenth Stowk, and also so much Hay. Proceed on through some Fields from which Dalton Town is in full View, and go over a Bridge. Entering Dalton, it is very clean, and, going a few more Paces, it is viewed with Pleasure; for it is like one of the Streets of London when one looks into a Shew Glass. Observe on thine right Hand a Sort of Pillar or Cross, seeming to be the chief Cross in the Town, which I think has been thought so formerly, but is not, I suppose, held now in so much Esteem. It is an old Saying, 'Dalton for a Kirk and a Castle'. There are 3 or 4 Inns at Dalton, namely these — the Red Lion, Thomas Strickland; the White Horse, but I do not know the Man's Name; and the King's Arms, William Thornton. But the grandest Place is Lord Stanley's Hunting Rooms; they indeed exceed some Rooms at Conishead. They are called so, because they are frequented by his Lordship every Year to a Hunt, and by several Gentlemen who accompany his Lordship. T. West says in his *Guide to the Lakes*, Page the 38, that the weekly Market hath long been established at Ulverstone to the Prejudice of Dalton. I dare say that the yearly Hunt at Dalton is a great Vexation to some of the Inhabitants of Ulverstone. I set off from Dalton a little after Dinner, being very impatient; because of not having Time enough to view such a remarkable Place.

About twenty years later in 1798, Barfoot and Wilkes described the town as follows in the *Universal British Directory*:

'*Dalton, Lancashire*. Is an ancient market town, situate about 257 miles north-north west of London . . . at the side of a rich vale, upon a fine lime-stone rock. On the west side of the market place there is an old tower or castle, built by the abbots of Furness . . . The landholders within the parish . . . are possessed of perhaps the finest and most fertile ground of any in the kingdom . . . The inhabitants within the parish of Dalton are more civilized and better informed than in many country towns; which is chiefly owing to four free grammar schools, and a monthly book-club, which has continued for many years in Dalton, whereby the best books in the English language are circulated among the parishioners at a small expence. It is somewhat remarkable, that there is not one family of dissenters throughout the whole parish . . .'.

Both these descriptions are mildly complimentary and give a generally pleasant impression of a typical, small country town, although by the end of the 18th century it was in fact beginning to show its age. The vicarage, for example was described in 1778 as being '. . . 9 yards in length and 6 yards in breadth, a mean old decayed building . . . built of limestone and covered with a very ordinary kind of slate . . .', and was doubtless the same building built by Anthony Turner 'out of the Ruines of an old house'. It is not known for certain when the church was built, but it was probably in the 15th or 16th century, and by this time was also showing signs of decay, assisted no doubt by the 17 years of neglect during the Commonwealth. It contained a 14th-century octagonal font, with two small shields on each of the seven sides, and on the eighth side one large shield on which was carved the original arms of Furness Abbey. This font can be seen today in a much weathered condition in the present church.

Ever since the later abbots of Furness lost interest in the upkeep of the castle it seems to have been frequently in need of repair, and at the beginning of the 19th century, when part of the ground floor was being used as a stable, it appears once again to be in a rather dilapidated condition. Cuitt's drawing (see p. 64) shows it as it appeared in 1817, with houses built on to its northern and eastern walls. The two houses attached to the front (eastern) side of the castle, were raised clear of the ground, supported on eight-foot tall stone pillars. The covered space beneath was used for a time as a shambles, or covered market. Not long before they were demolished, their occupants were James Kendall, a painter, who painted a view of the castle, and 'Aggie' Palmer. Two of the stone columns were used in the porch of the offices constructed on this site in 1850–51 by a solicitor, Mr. William Butler. When this building was demolished in 1896, the columns were removed to the front door of Bank House, in Church Street, where they may still be seen today.

A short row of four houses extended from the north side of the castle. Immediately adjacent was a three-storey house which had been occupied in 1840 by Bella Woodend, and in 1858 by William Barben. Next to this were two smaller houses, the first one having been occupied by Robert Helm, and the second by Miss Lawrence, the post-mistress, who lived there with her sister and brother-in-law, Mr. Wilson, who was the excise officer. The occupant of the end house was Matthew Robinson, stonemason and town crier in 1849. These houses were all demolished sometime after 1858.[2] Many of the houses on Market Place at this time must have been quite respectable, having been built less than a century earlier, but no doubt replacing earlier ones which had existed on the same site.

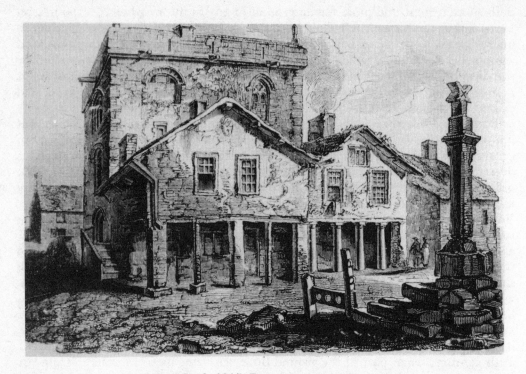

15. Dalton Castle 1817. From an engraving by G. Cuitt.

At least one of the houses dated from the 17th century; this is the old *Ship Inn*, easily recognised today because it bears the date 1683 on its wall. Another house nearby, No. 3 Market Street, is reputed to have been built about 1570, and if this is correct it must be the oldest house in Dalton.

The old St Andrew's cross had stood for centuries in front of the castle, its condition, as portrayed by Cuitt, unmistakably neglected. This also is likely to have been a direct consequence of the Commonwealth, some two centuries earlier, when so many ancient crosses throughout the land were deliberately damaged or destroyed. It was repaired in 1824, and again in 1843, and finally replaced by the present cross in 1869 when the fish-stones were also erected. The stocks and whipping post were situated close to the south-east corner of the cross. In 1856 the stocks were removed by the simple expedient of cutting through the wooden legs, leaving the stumps in the ground; and three years later, the whipping post suffered a similar fate. About ten years after this, when work on the new cross had started, the buried stumps, which were made of oak were dug up, and the vicar, the Rev. J. M. Morgan, used them for firewood.

The condition of the castle has already been commented upon. It was described by William Close, about 1804. 'The ground floor is divided into two apartments.

The principal entrance into the edifice at present is by a small door in the west side, from whence a spiral staircase ascends to the room where the Courts for the Liberty of Furness are held . . . From the courtroom the stairs lead to a room above, and to the top of the castle which is surrounded by a parapet . . . The highest apartment is lighted by the great window and the court-room by the window below. The great door on the same side has been the ancient entrance; the small doorway on the west side has been broke through the wall (about 1704) in order to enter directly into the spiral staircase. The apartment immediately within the great door was, about a century ago . . . converted into a stable, but the doorway leading from the ancient entrance to the bottom of the spiral staircase is still visible in an interior wall. At the foot of the stairs there is a deep (5 ft 6 in) excavation called the dungeon, which appears to have had a room over it on a level with the ground floor of the adjoining apartment (the stable). This higher room has been lighted by a small aperture on the north side, but that below (the dungeon) has been completely dark, and is thought to have been a cell appropriated for the reception of prisoners. The ground plan of this edifice is an oblong square; the east and west sides measuring 45 feet, the north and south, 30 feet'. This, then, is a brief description of the town's principal physical characteristics before its mid-century transformation into a much larger industrial town. Merryweather's map of 1825 shows its total size, and many features which have now disappeared entirely or been drastically altered. It clearly illustrates that at this time Dalton was a very small agricultural town.

How the town changed

The effects of the mining industry on the town's size and economy were many and varied, and can only be briefly considered here. Let us begin by referring once again to Merryweather's map. About half a mile to the east of the castle, at the opposite end of Market Street, is Tudor Square. On the map it is unnamed, but may easily be identified by its prominent triangular shape. On Hogenberg's map of 1577 it is shown as 'Town End', thus suggesting the existence of a village-type settlement, separate from but administratively part of Dalton, with its houses and farms almost certainly occupying the same building-line as the present-day houses and shops. According to W. G. Hoskins,[3] many medieval villages developed around an enclosed space, the village green, in which the livestock could be confined at night-time for safety. This is quite possibly what happened here; the word 'green' seems to have persisted throughout the years, even as recently as 1948, when a triangular plot of land behind the row of houses Nos. 1-4, was always referred to as 'the green' by the locals. Hoskins also mentions that many of these villages had a back lane enclosing part of the site. Many older Daltonians will confirm that Beckside Road, in local parlance, was often referred to as the back lane. All this evidence, although tenuous to say the least, does at least point to the possibility that what today is a busy bus terminus, centuries ago was a rustic village green.

In the 19th century, however, this area came to be known as Bally Green, and is shown as such on the 1842 tithe map. Attempts to determine the origin of

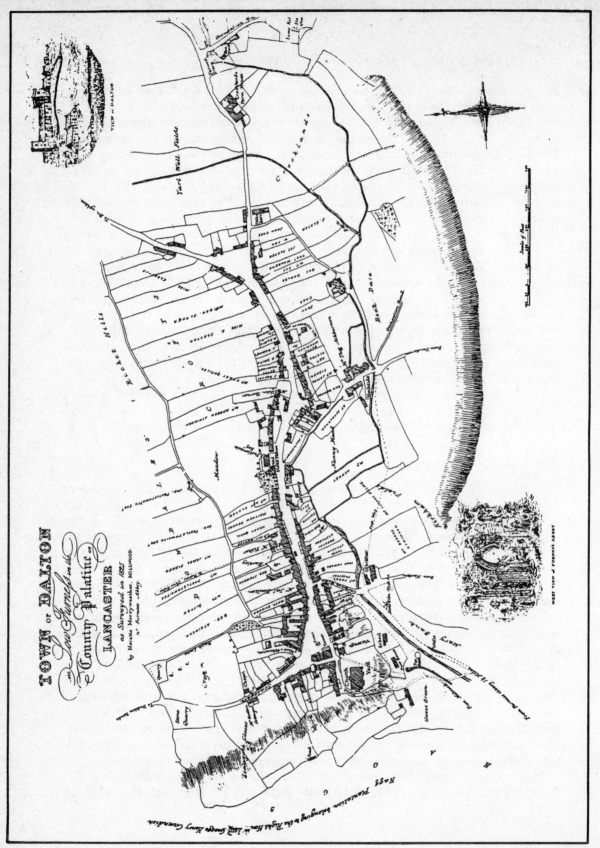

16. Map of Dalton in 1825 as surveyed by Horatio Merryweather.

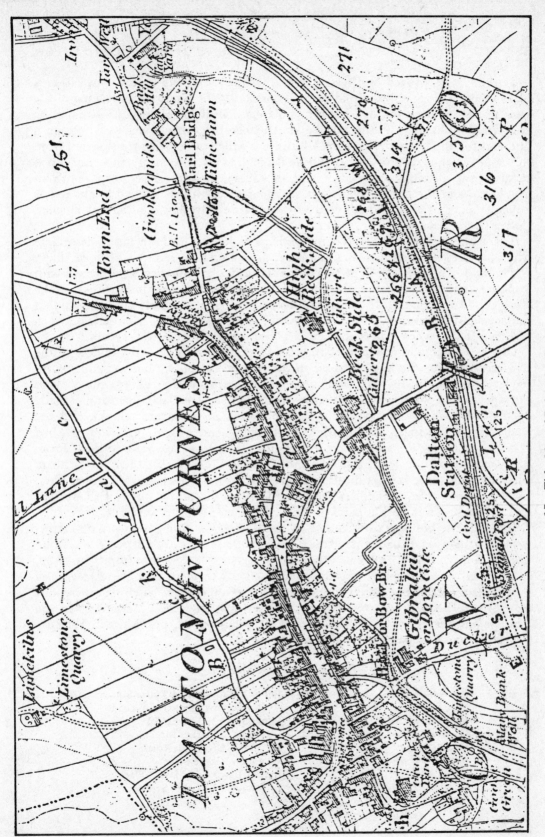

17. Tithe Map of Dalton in 1842.

this name have proved fruitless. James Melville[4] suggests that it was either a place where ball games were played, or, considering the alternative meaning of the word 'ball', a place for dancing (Maypole e.g.). Both these suggestions must be considered unlikely. By the middle of the century, the Green had become a junction for the horse-drawn carts of iron-ore which were being transported from the mines around the town, to the docks at Barrow. Inevitably this traffic was carried on in all kinds of weather, and, of course, the rain caused seepage of red-iron-ore from the carts. The rutted, churned-up earth was stained bright red as a consequence of this, and resulted in the area being rather cynically nicknamed 'Never Green Square'.

This name is interesting and could perhaps be important in trying to determine when the present name was first adopted, as it contains elements of both 'Bally Green' and 'Tudor Square'. If this name has any chronological significance with respect to the present name, then it could be interpreted as an indication that the change to 'Tudor Square' took place rather earlier than is generally believed. All that can be said with certainty, however, is that the name was changed sometime between 1842 and 1886, when it first appears as Tudor Square in a local directory.[5]

One inevitable consequence of the town's transformation in the middle of the 19th century was the large increase in the number of public houses; an amenity rendered necessary by the large number of permanently thirsty miners who came to live in the town at this time. In Barfoot and Wilkes,[6] mention is made of the *White Horse* (John Cartmel), the *Red Lion* (Margaret Cook), and the *King's Arms* (Richard Thornton); but strangely there is no mention of *Lord Stanley's Hunting Rooms*, or the *Cavendish Arms* as it was later known. From the same source we learn that the proprietor of the *Punch Bowl* was William Gill, although there is no indication where this property was situated. Altogether, there are nine other victuallers mentioned in this directory, but it is likely that some of these were in other parts of the parish — two at least were in Barrow.

In 1825, the building now known as the *Wellington Hotel* is shown on Merry-weather's map as Broadstone House. By 1849, it was called the *Broadstone Hotel*,[7] and in 1855 its name was changed to the *Wellington Hotel*. In 1829, apart from the older pubs already mentioned, there were also the *George and Dragon* (situated immediately opposite the parish church gates — now rebuilt as a private house), and the *Plough*, whose location is now unknown. In the *History and Directory of Furness and West Cumberland*, published in 1882 by P. Mannex and Company, the following are listed:

Hotels, Inns and Taverns

Black Bull	James Thompson, 14 Tudor Square
Bridge Inn	Arthur Barrow, Broughton Road
Britannia Hotel	James Spence, Ann Street
Cavendish Arms	J. Hepple, 3 Market Street
Clarence Hotel	Rd. Clark, Ulverston Road
George and Dragon	M. Askew, Castle Street
King's Arms	Jno. St Lawrence, Market Place
Masons' Arms	J. Holmes, 91 Market Street

White Horse Inn,

DALTON.

TO BE SOLD,

UPON THE PREMISES,

On FRIDAY the 15th DAY of DECEMBER, 1809,

AT 6 O'CLOCK IN THE EVENING;

ALL that commodious and well accustomed **PUBLIC HOUSE**, commonly known by the

Sign of the White Horse,

Situate in Dalton, in the County of Lancaster, consisting of a large House, three Parlours, excellent Cellars, Kitchen and Brew-house, large Dining Room and convenient Bed Rooms, with Stabling for 10 Horses and a Garden adjoining, all in complete Repair, and may be entered upon at May-day next.

Also, a very good Garden situate at the head of Dow-KER LANE, near Dalton aforesaid.

And a Close of excellent arable Ground called

MARY BANK PARROCK,

by Estimation 1 Acre Statute Measure.

The above Premises are held of the Manor of Dalton, by payment of the Yearly Rent of 2s. 9½d. and a fine of only 3s. 4d. upon Change of Tenant.

¶ Mr. John Gardner the Owner, will shew the Premises, of whom further Particulars may be had, or by applying to Mr. Atkinson at Dalton aforesaid.

18. Public house sale poster.

Hotels, Inns and Taverns — continued

Prince of Wales	Geo. Wilson, Broughton Road
Railway Arms	Wm. Hodgson, Station Road
Red Lion Inn	Eliz. Denney, Market Street
Ship Inn	Thos. Turner, 5 Market Place
Wellington Hotel	Fred Bell, Market Street
White Horse Inn	J. Holmes, 6 Market Street

Beerhouses

Bow Bridge	James Barben
Brown Cow	Wm. Brand, Goose Green
Devonshire Arms	Robert Remington, Albert Street
Farmer's Arms	T. Shuttleworth, 33 Market Street
Fountain Head	Benjamin Sweetman, Stafford Street
Golden Ball	John Hardy, 15 Tudor Square
Horse and Jockey	Jos. Shaw, Ulverston Road
Joiners' Arms	Thos. Robinson, Devonshire Street
Melton Hotel	Robert Mason
Miners' Arms	Rd. Metcalf, Ulverston Road
Old House at Home	George Greave, Skellgate
Sun Inn	David Murphy, Broughton Road.

Obviously the oldest pubs in the town today are the *White Horse*, the *Cavendish Arms* and the *Red Lion*. It is possible that the *Brown Cow* is also very ancient; but attempts to determine the age of all these pubs from the property deeds have proved fruitless, because it seems that all the old documents appertaining to them have been lost or are otherwise inaccessible. This is certainly the case with the *White Horse*; and the earliest surviving deed for the *Cavendish* dates from only 1870. It is obvious that all these pubs are much older than this.

An interesting feature of the *Cavendish* is the large hole which exists beneath the floor-boards of the function room at the rear of the building. This hole is several feet in diameter, with straight, completely vertical sides which have been neatly plastered. It seems as though at one time it might have been a well, although why it should be so large is difficult to imagine. It is now partly filled with rubble. The discovery of another well in the cellar of the same pub was reported in the *Dalton News* on 14 August 1915. 'A well which has existed in the cellar of the *Cavendish Arms* for several centuries, has been re-discovered. No living person was aware of its existence, and it was only brought to light through the breaking of a flagstone during some structural alterations which Mr. Dixon, the landlord, was having effected this week. Mr. Comber, who was doing the work, found the well, and on testing it, ascertained that it was about eight feet deep and full of a gas which extinguished a candle as soon as it was lowered into the well. The idea is that the well was connected with the Castle, as the *Cavendish Arms* is nearly as old as that edifice, documents existing to prove that it is at least 600 years old. In its early days the hotel was known as the *Black Cock*, the custom then being to name such places after wild animals or birds. During the occupancy of Mr. Dixon the presence of such an ancient well was never suspected'. It is a pity that this newspaper article does not identify the documents which purport to render the *Black Cock* as being almost coeval with the castle. Subsequent searching has failed to throw any fresh light on the subject. This, of course, does not necessarily mean that the documents referred to do not exist, or have never existed, and, if this report is true, then the present pub could well be regarded as the oldest in the town. No doubt the structure has been altered over the years, and one must accept the possibility that the *Black Cock* was an entirely different building occupying the same site. During the summer of 1981, the interior of the *Cavendish Arms* was substantially rebuilt, and, although the alterations have imparted to it an air of pseudo-antiquity, the truly ancient character of the old pub has now disappeared.

Although over the years the external structure of the *White Horse* has been altered, it seems that the cellar has hardly been touched and its antiquity is immediately obvious. The larger part of the cellar is directly beneath the bar; but the most interesting part is the stone-built, bow-ceilinged smaller room which appears to project beyond the building line and out beneath the pavement. There is a vague sort of tradition that long ago, this was a place of punishment and miscreants were brought here to be whipped. Whether or not this story has any foundation in fact it is now impossible to say; but it does seem to be unlikely because, until well into the 19th century, the whipping post still existed just a short distance away, outside the castle.

The *Red Lion* appears to have no particular claim to fame other than the fact that, according to the dramatist Richard Cumberland, who was writing about the young George Romney (*see* pp. 90-93), there was a painting of a red lion adorning the exterior of the inn and this must have been Romney's first visual inspiration in the art of painting. The point is interesting because this information can only have come from Romney himself, and must inevitably mean that he had stood outside and examined the sign, and possibly that from time to time he even visited the inn as a customer.

Although the increase in the number of public houses was a direct result of the expanding population, there can be no doubt that the most dramatic effect that the local iron-ore mines had on the town was its rapid increase in size — a phenomenon which the authorities were not really equipped to cope with at that time. Rows of houses which had been built with little or no regard to sanitation soon became slums. The disgraceful state of affairs existing in Dalton in the 19th century is vividly portrayed in a report to the Local Board presented by Mr. W. H. Fox, the surveyor, which was reported in the *Ulverston Mirror* on 20 December 1873. Some extracts from this report are given here:

Over one thousand houses had been visited, 938 being habited dwellings. Ten thousand notes and observations as to the sanitary state had been chronicled, and to assist the members of the board at arriving at some general idea of the sanitary state of the town, examples were given from the inspection book. No names, however, were mentioned, as where so much sanitary evil existed it would have been invidious to give several offenders only. In some instances the wretched, unhealthy state of the dwellings was due to the landlords, in others to the tenants, but in the majority undoubtedly to the want of house accommodation, clean roads and pavements, good sewerage, and an efficient system for the removal of refuse. Market Street and Tudor Square showed house drainage for liquid refuse of all kinds by an open channel into the street, thence to gullies to the main sewer. Some of the water was thrown into large open middens. The disgusting effect of this, especially in summer, would not be difficult to imagine. Pigstyes abounded as in many of the other streets, some in a filthy condition, and near the back doors of dwellings . . . In Bankside the houses were not provided with sufficient watertaps, and a single tap had to provide 14 dwellings. The inconvenience required no comment. In some houses the tenants kept fowls, and other unsuitable tenants, which made the house filthy. At Bricklane forty persons slept in twelve very small bedrooms. In Stafford Street 33 persons were living in three small cottages. In Butt's Cottages one convenience was provided for 44 persons, and one water tap served twenty houses. In Devonshire Street five persons were sleeping in one bedroom, 11 feet by 8 and 8 feet in height . . .

Although this paints a pretty dismal picture of 19th-century Dalton, it must be pointed out that not all the town was like this — the older parts in particular remained very respectable. It must also be emphasised that, in Furness, these problems were not unique to Dalton; both Barrow and Ulverston had their less salubrious areas too in which conditions were equally as bad as those described here. Although the physical increase in the size of the town was the most obvious effect of the growth of the mining industry, the growing importance of the town necessitated the establishment of various public utility services.

The Post Office

Furness postal history began with the opening of the post office at Ulverston in 1793. This office served the whole rural area, including Dalton. Subsequently there was a foot post to Dalton and Barrow, leaving Ulverston at 6.45 a.m., the carrier walking to Dalton and on to Barrow, delivering and collecting on the way. He returned to Ulverston at 5 p.m. Dalton became part of the Ulverston Penny Post in 1836, so, presumably there was a 'receiving house' in Dalton. An ornate stamp, 'No. 5', was allotted and this was applied in red ink from 1836 until 1840 when the Penny Post was introduced. In 1841 Dalton was issued with a neat, undated circular stamp which was also applied in red, but in later years, from 1844 onwards, was applied in blue. The foot post continued until 1869, from which time the railway was used.

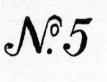

(a)   (b)

19. Early postmarks: (a) Handstamp. Used from 1836–40. (b) Undated stamp. 1841 onwards. By courtesy of Mr. Ernest Boddy.

It is reported that in 1858 the post office at Dalton was situated in one of four cottages built against the north wall of the castle. Miss Mary Lawrence was the postmistress, and she shared the house with her sister and brother-in-law. Some time after 1858, these houses were demolished, and the post office was moved either to a house nearby in Castle Street, or to the site now occupied by the Electricity Board showroom at number 73, Market Street. There can be no doubt that this is where the post office was situated in 1876 when the postmaster was Mr. Christopher Godby.[8] From a number of letters in the contemporary press, it is quite obvious that during Mr. Godby's term of office, the postal arrangements left much to be desired. A gentleman signing himself 'Progress', writing in the *Dalton News*, 9 May 1885, complains that there is no postal delivery to the outlying areas of the town; but perhaps the most informative and interesting account of conditions at that time is contained in the following letter published one week earlier in the same newspaper:

> Sir, I have been much struck with the inconvenience the public suffer in consequence of the very defective structural arrangements at the Post Office. There is no proper desk provided for writing telegrams, the shop counter only being the miserable substitute for that much needed commodity. Consequently, when writing a telegram, the sender has the privilege of being overlooked by the congregation of persons standing around him ... Further, it is high time that telegrams could be sent, and stamps purchased from the hour of opening to the hour of closing the office. Under present regulations a telegram can only be sent after the clock has struck eight in the morning, although the office has been open at least an hour before that time, and postage stamps can only be purchased up to eight o'clock in the evening, although the post does not close until half-past eight ... I have observed an unfortunate victim standing by the letter box after eight o'clock in the evening, begging of a passer-by to sell him a stamp to enable him to post his letter. Trusting the tyrannical regulations imposed on the inhabitants of Dalton by the Postal Authorities, will be promptly regulated in accordance with the progressive spirit of the age, and accommodation afforded as in other towns, I beg to subscribe myself, your obedient servant.

In September 1885, local ratepayers petitioned the postal authorities in London, complaining of the unsatisfactory accommodation in the post office, and requesting that a new building be erected for the purpose on the vacant plot of land at the corner of Station Road (formerly occupied by the malt kiln). Although this petition must have been considered by the authorities, it is obvious that no action was taken other than perhaps modest improvements to the existing office; another 40 years was to elapse before the post office was finally to be moved.

Breweries

One result of the town's increasing population was the establishment of two breweries in the 19th century. One of them, the Dalton Brewery, seems to have been in existence since at least 1844, on the site in Market Street presently occupied by the Roxy bingo hall. The other one, the Beckside Brewery, situated at High Beckside must have been established at about the same time, but the precise date is not certain. Little seems to have been written about either brewery, but from the number of times they were advertised in the local newspapers as being for sale, a general impression is that from the 1860s onwards, they were not showing a worthwhile profit. Originally, however, the Dalton Brewery at least must have flourished, for its owner Mr. Matthew Denney soon acquired the ownership or substantial leases of several public houses and malt-kilns in the area including: the *Anchor* (Lindal); the *Miners' Arms* (Stainton); the *Brewer's Arms* and a cottage on Skelgate; the *Railway Arms*; the *Lancaster Arms*; and the *Lord Nelson* with two adjoining cottages.

It may be that Mr. Denney's troubles began with what must have been a disastrous fire in September 1869. At this time there was no fire-brigade in Dalton and the Barrow appliance was called out. It was reported as follows to the Gas and Water Committee of the Borough of Barrow:

> An alarm of fire was given at the Station about 1 o'clock on Saturday morning last: the fire was out of the Borough, upon the premises of Mr. Matthew Denny, Brewer, Dalton. We left at 1.30, and had the engine at work in 35 minutes after. We had a plentiful supply of water and good assistance from volunteer leaver-men. The roof of the building was totally destroyed when we arrived and the whole contents, consisting of hay, straw, etc., were in one body of fire. In about an hour the fire was so much under as to enable us to stop the engine. At daylight I had all the hot hay etc. removed. and stood by the engine in case of outbreak which did sometimes occur. At 7 o'clock the place was cleared and no sign of any fire: we returned to the station at 8 o'clock with 4 buckets short. which I hope will be found. The engine worked remarkably well: we had not the slightest accident or breakdown. The Brigade were wanting for nothing and also worked very steady.

On 28 March 1899, all the loose brewing plant and equipment belonging to the Beckside Brewery was sold by auction, and from this date the brewery ceased to exist. Seven attempts were made to dispose of the Dalton Brewery in the last 40 years of its existence, and it was finally disposed of in 1909 when it was bought by the Dalton Urban District Council to be demolished as part of a road-widening scheme.

The Furness Railway

Although it cannot be claimed that the local iron industry was solely responsible for the formation of the Furness Railway, the fact that large quantities of iron-ore had to be transported from the mines to the coast was an important contributory factor in the final decision to proceed with the plan. On 23 May 1844, the Furness Railway Act was passed by Parliament, with an authorised capital of £100,000. J. & W. Tredwell were the contractors, but as labour was difficult to recruit the original estimate of £47,789 was increased to £67,000.

By 1846, the line which extended from Kirkby to Rampside with a branch to Dalton had been opened with the minimum of ceremony. It was not until April 1854 that the railway reached Ulverston, little over four miles from Dalton. This seemingly long time was due to severe difficulties encountered by the contractors, Messrs. Boulton of Leeds in the construction of the tunnel at Lindal, and also because many of the townspeople of Ulverston strongly opposed the idea of the railway entering their town.

As may be expected, the railway brought its share of mishaps. Referring once again to William Fisher's diary:

May 10, 1846	Henry Houghton a youth of 16 years of age unfortunately fell under one of the Wagons on furness Railway and had his legs so much crushed that he died a few days after of inflamation.
Jul. 16, 1846	Wm. Wilson a labourer for furness Railway 22 years of age who through inadvertance had placed himself betwixt two Waggons one of which [was] moving when his knee was caught betwixt them which cosed a compound fracture ending in mortification and died 7 days after.
Nov. 18, 1847	Killed on the Dalton Railway a man named Spence by 3 waggons running over him breaking both his thighs he died about 2 hours after.
Nov. 6, 1855	2 men working in Lindal Railway Tunnel when a blast exploded Killed one and sadly injured the other so that his life was dispaired of.

Shortly after the line through Dalton was opened (1846), the company realised that they would have to provide some form of accommodation for passengers while they were waiting for trains. The original station would have been a simple wooden affair close to the site of the present one, but as passenger traffic increased, the present structure was built from locally hewn sandstone and limestone. The style is typical of many Furness stations with the steep pitched roofs, described by the Company as the Swiss Cottage style.

As built, the station had two through platforms, capable of accommodating the longest trains, and two bays, one at the east and one at the west ends of the station. These were for the use of local workmen's trains, such as were common until the 1930s, and until the motor bus took over. A commodious goods yard was provided on the south side of the line. This yard had coal and cattle wharfs, and a weighbridge. It served the needs of many local traders in the days before road transport became popular. Ornate cast iron canopies were provided, and gas for lighting was supplied by the town's works at Goose Green. For many years, the only method of crossing from one platform to another was via a wooden level crossing over the rails at the east end of the station, by the present road bridge. However, after an unpleasant accident in the 1870s, when a man paused to pick up a farthing he had dropped on the crossing, and was struck down by a train coasting down the hill from Lindal thus losing both his legs, the company extended the overbridge and constructed a pedestrian way over the lines.

Many local people will remember Abbotswood, a neo-Gothic mansion which formerly stood just outside the town of Dalton, close to Mill Brow and over-looked the Vale of Nightshade and the ruins of Furness Abbey; but they may not be aware of its association with the Furness Railway. It was about 1845 when Mr. James Ramsden was appointed manager of the engineering department. He was then about 23 years old, but despite his youth, quickly established himself as a capable and efficient man. By 1857 he had become so indispensable to the

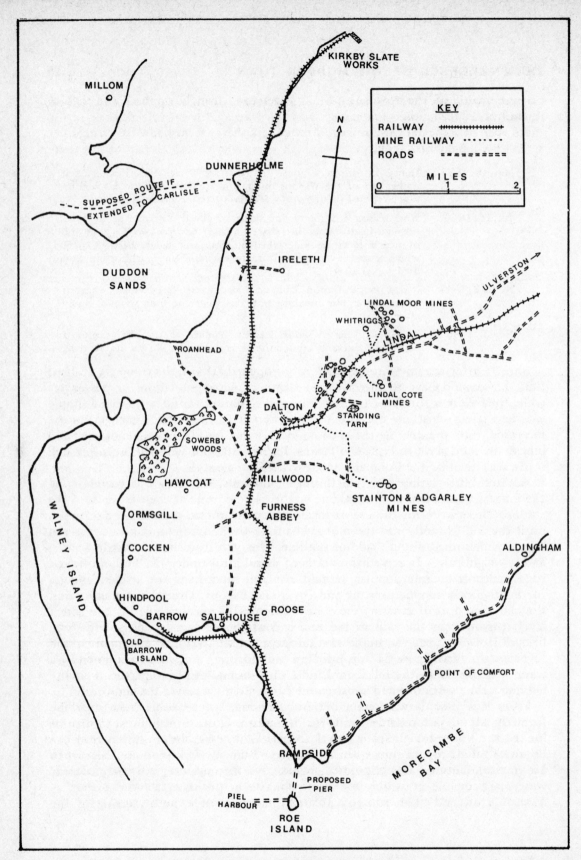

MILLOM

KIRKBY SLATE
WORKS

KEY

RAILWAY
MINE RAILWAY
ROADS

MILES
0   1   2

DUNNERHOLME

SUPPOSED ROUTE IF
EXTENDED TO CARLISLE

IRELETH

ULVERSTON

DUDDON
SANDS

LINDAL MOOR MINES

WHITRIGGS

LINDAL

ROANHEAD

LINDAL COTE
MINES

DALTON

STANDING
TARN

SOWERBY
WOODS

STAINTON & ADGARLEY
MINES

HAWCOAT

MILLWOOD

FURNESS
ABBEY

ORMSGILL

WALNEY ISLAND

COCKEN

ALDINGHAM

HINDPOOL

BARROW   SALTHOUSE   ROOSE

OLD
BARROW
ISLAND

POINT OF COMFORT

RAMPSIDE

MORECAMBE
BAY

PROPOSED
PIER

PIEL
HARBOUR

ROE
ISLAND

20. Proposed route of Furness Railway, 1843.

Company, that it was resolved to build a residence for him on the site described. A sum of £2,000 was to be spent and Mr. Ramsden was to be allowed to live there at a rent of 2 per cent of the outlay.

The land belonged to the Earl of Burlington who was Chairman of the Company, and who was responsible for the erection of this magnificent mansion, with its square towers, beautiful gardens four lodges, coach-house, stable, greenhouses and a small home farm. The sandstone used in its construction was brought from Hawcoat quarry. Mr. Ramsden was in occupation by about 1865. He never actually owned Abbotswood, instead he paid a yearly rent of £205, indicating that the value of the site was close to £10,000. He was knighted in 1872, and lived there until his death in 1896. His widow died the following year. After changing hands a number of times, the property was finally demolished in the 1960s.

The Gasworks

The first step in the establishment of a gasworks in the town took place on 16 April 1852, when at a meeting of property owners from the Division of Dalton Proper which was held in the vestry of the parish church, an executive committee consisting of seven gentlemen was appointed to supervise the building and management of the proposed gasworks. It was also resolved that the gas should be used for lighting the town, and that the gasworks should belong completely to the Division of Dalton Proper. The capital outlay for this project was realised through the sale to the Furness Railway Company, of certain common and waste lands in the Division of Dalton Proper, and a sum of approximately £700 was set aside for this purpose.

Under the direction of the committee, the gasworks was ultimately built on a piece of land formerly known as Mary Bank (near Goose Green and now the site of a car saleroom), which had been presented to the township of Dalton by the Furness Railway Company, and by a deed dated 10 October 1853 was conveyed to the executive committee, to be held by them 'their heirs and assigns for ever, to be appropriated and used as and for a site of Gas Works for the town and neighbourhood of Dalton-in-Furness aforesaid'. Gas mains were laid and street lamps provided by the committee, and a considerable portion of the town was lighted free of further cost to the ratepayers until October 1871, when the Lighting and Watching Act was adopted and Lighting Inspectors appointed, by whom further lamps were erected, and who continued the supervision of the lighting of the town until 1873, when the Local Board assumed this responsibility.

From this time onwards, there were a number of serious attempts by the Local Board to purchase the gasworks; the first one was under the authority of the Dalton-in-Furness District Local Board Act, 1878, which empowered the Board to purchase and subsequently dispose of the gasworks and site, but not to use or manufacture gas at the existing works. For this purpose, two new gasworks were planned; one of which was to be situated at Crooklands and the other at Askam. This, and other subsequent attempts to transfer the ownership of the works to the Local Board, was not successful, and the authority conferred upon the Local Board by this particular Act was allowed to lapse.

It is interesting in today's climate of constantly rising prices, to observe that, in the first fifteen years, the price of gas manufactured at the Dalton works fell almost steadily. The following table tells its own story:

Year	Price per 1,000 cubic feet	Year	Price per 1,000 cubic feet
1873–7	7s. 6d.	1880–1	4s. 2d.
1877–8	6s. 8d.	1881–3	5s. 0d.
1878–9	5s. 0d.	1883–5	4s. 7d.
1879–80	4s. 2d.	1886–7	3s. 9d.

Eventually, however, the transfer of ownership was completed; yet, surprisingly this did not take place until well into the present century. On 18 December 1935, a public meeting was held for the ratepayers of the town to approve or reject the latest terms for the Council to purchase the works. The result was that the terms and conditions were approved, and an Act of Parliament was invoked in 1936, conferring upon the Dalton Urban District Council the necessary powers to effect the purchase of the site, and to continue the manufacture of gas. The change of ownership took place on 1 October 1936, and lasted until 1948, when the old gasworks finally closed down.

The Cemetery

Although no-one knows then the graveyard adjoining the parish church was first consecrated as a burial ground, it was certainly a long time ago; perhaps as far back as the eighth or ninth century A.D., but almost certainly coeval with the introduction of Christianity into Furness. For almost the whole period of its existence this graveyard must have been the only one in the town, and from the parish registers we can calculate that it must have catered for something like 4,000 burials per century. In the last century, the influx of miners from different parts of the country brought various nonconformist groups to the town, and it is possible that many of them used their own burial grounds. It is rumoured for example that the gardens behind the two houses on Skelgate which were once the Methodist Chapel, mark the site of their graveyard.

Obviously however, the rather small parish churchyard became so overcrowded that no such thing as a discreet and private burial would have been possible without disturbing the remains of the former parishioners, and in 1860, in pursuance of an Order in Council, it was decreed that the parish churchyard should be closed for interments. At the same time a Burial Board consisting of nine members was formed. On 14 February 1861, they purchased from the trustees of Joseph Ormandy a piece of land called Mary Bank Close for the purpose of providing a new cementery. For the same purpose, on 27 October 1862, they also purchased King's Close from the Furness Railway Company. Upon this latter plot of land they erected a board room (situated, it was said, on the site of the cockpit), a registrar's residence, out-offices, a hearse-house and a mortuary chapel.

According to Tyson (*Dalton Local Board Accounts 1882–1896*) 'The Chapel and Cemetery ground (except the portion reserved for Nonconformists) were consecrated by the late Lord Bishop (Waldegrave) of Carlisle, on the 1st November, 1862 . . . The first interment in the Cemetery was that of Mrs. Elizabeth White, on the 3rd November, 1862 . . . In consequence of the increasing population and the urgent necessity for additional burial accommodation the Board purchased, on the 8th September, 1871, from Mr. Matthew Denney, 4 acres of land abutting on the south side of the Cemetery, to which the same was added, and on this land was erected a second mortuary chapel, which is allotted to the use of Nonconformists. The Church of England portion of the additional land was consecrated by the present Lord Bishop (Goodwin) of Carlisle, on the 18th March, 1872 . . . Up to the year 1875, the inhabitants of Barrow had the right of Burial at the Dalton Cemetery, but in pursuance of the Barrow-in-Furness Corporation Act, 1875, sec. 119, upon payment by the Corporation of £2,700 to the Board, all rights and interests of the parishioners or inhabitants of the Borough of Barrow, in respect of the Dalton Burial Board, or their Cemetery or property (other than private rights of burial) ceased as from the 31st October, 1875, and the Corporation (under the authority of the Corporation Act, 1873, sec. 40) agreed to pay, in addition to the sum above mentioned, an annuity of £75 to the Vicar of Dalton, and £12 10s. per annum to the then Parish Clerk in respect of burial fees'.

In July 1973, a 1.2 acre extension to the Church of England section of the cemetery was consecrated by the Bishop of Penrith who, making the sign of the Cross on the ground with his staff, said 'we mark this ground with the symbol of our most holy faith and hereby consecrate it to be the resting place of the faithful'.

The Fire Brigade

It was reported in the minute book of the Dalton Local Board, that at a meeting held on 2 March 1874 it was decided that 'The Committee recommend that a Fire Brigade be formed and that the Hydrants be tested at least once a quarter, and that the men be paid 2s. 6d. each time for their services and that Mr. William Rawlinson be the Captain, and Mr. Edward Mitchell the Hydrant man'. This marks the beginning of the town's first official fire brigade; although it seems that for some time before 1874, there had been a fire-fighting appliance of some sort in the hands of the Gas Committee.

The newly-formed Dalton fire brigade did not last very long, for the following year in September 1875, there was some disagreement between the brigade and the Local Board which culminated in the resignation of the entire brigade. Mr. E. B. Mitchell, who was by this time Captain of the fire brigade, wrote: 'The Dalton Local Board at their meeting on Monday, the 6th inst., passed a resolution to the effect that the Fire Brigade when out practising with the hose on the evening of August 6th, had not carried out their duty by not properly testing the various hydrants, and therefore each member of the brigade received only half his usual pay, that is 1s. 3d. instead of 2s. 6d. One member of the board had gone so far as to say that only one hydrant was used, whereas nine were tested and used and then further practice was impossible through very heavy rain falling. The result is that I, as the captain, and the rest that formed the brigade have resigned, determined not to be any longer governed by two or three people, that are set in motion by Mr. J. Robinson'. At the council meeting following this incident, the letter of resignation was read out, and, after some discussion, the Lighting and Watching Committee were instructed to take steps to form another brigade.

In 1885, when the Local Board moved from Market Place to its new offices in Station Road, the horses for both the fire brigade and the ambulance were stabled at the rear of the new premises. At about the turn of the century, the horsemen for both the fire brigade and the ambulance services was Mr. Welstead, who came from London. He was also the driver of the ambulance. At first he had charge of three horses; one of them, a grey, was called Sidebones, and later, another horse, Darkie, was purchased for the rather high price of £90. There are several old Daltonians still living who can testify to the fact that the horses were so well trained that, when the fire bell started ringing and they were released from the stable, they would trot across the yard and position themselves on either side of the shaft of the appliance.

The fire-engine was kept in a state of instant readiness with its boiler full of water and the fire laid, so that it just required a match to light it. To see the fire-engine careering at speed along the rough streets, with sparks flying from the horses' hooves and the crew clinging to the swaying vehicle was a sight which never failed to attract crowds of spectators. One of its most famous captains was 'mad Captain Dunne' who earned himself this title because of the reckless speed at which he drove the horses.

Local Government

Throughout the 18th century when Dalton was just a small town with a large parish, local affairs (i.e. education, poor relief, the workhouse, maintenance of highways, etc.) were firmly controlled by the Four and Twenty. This was the nearest thing to organised local government at that time. By the middle of the 19th century, however, even though the population of the town of Dalton was increasing rapidly, Barrow's expansion was even more spectacular, and on 13 June 1867 the district of Barrow-in-Furness was incorporated as a Municipal Borough with a clearly defined boundary by royal charter. This was the first step in the dissection of the parish of Dalton, and was soon to lead to the final demise of the Four and Twenty. Further stages in the dismemberment of the parish followed quickly.

On 1 May 1871, under a Provisional Order made by the Poor Law Board, it was ordered that so much of the parish of Dalton as was comprised in the municipal borough of Barrow, together with Walney Island, Sheep Island, Piel Island, Foulney Island and surrounding waters and scars, sands, marshes etc., should, as from 29 December 1871 be separated from the parish of Dalton and should constitute a distinct place under the name of the Borough of Barrow. On 31 October 1875, the municipal borough of Barrow was extended to include a further portion of the township or Division of Yarlside. Three years later, on 12 August 1878, by order of the Local Government Board, certain other parts of the parish of Dalton, known as the Chapelry of Rampside, were amalgamated with the parish of Barrow.

The establishment of a Local Government Board for Dalton was proposed in 1873 and was eventually brought about, due largely to the efforts and influence of the directors of the Askam Ironworks. It occupied an office building situated on the east side of the castle, which had originally been built in 1851 by a solicitor, Mr. William Butler. The parish was divided into three wards — East, North and South, and each ward elected six members. The Board appointed its own medical officer, surveyor, treasurer, collector, market and nuisance inspector, and clerk, and held its meetings on the last Monday of each month at 2 p.m. In 1885 it moved to the new town hall in Station Road, where it survived until December, 1894, after which time the town council system of local government was introduced.

A more complete description of the workings of the Local Board is to be found in Tyson's *Dalton Local Board Accounts 1882–1896*, a copy of which is in the Local Collection at Barrow Library. The last Local Board meeting was held in December, 1894, and in January, 1895, the same members were all re-elected, together with two additional members, to form the first town council. The first chairman of the Dalton Town Council was Mr. J. W. Lawn, and its members were William Brocklebank, gentleman; James Butcher, engine driver; John Dixon, blacksmith; Lewis Olliver, grocer; W. Geo. Ashburner, brewer; Joseph Fisher, farmer; Arthur Waiting, manager; Oliver Bartlett, insurance agent; William Lewney, miner; Joseph Scannel, inland revenue officer; Charles Kirkbride, grocer; Sam. Challoner, surgeon; James Hamer, mines manager; James Towers, miner; Thomas Cowan, mining agent; John Johnson, ironmonger; John Wardley, bootmaker (retired); John Lawn, mines manager; John Myers, secretary; and John Wharton, aerated water manufacturer.

One beneficial consequence of the post-1850 population increase was that the market was revitalised. By 1881 however, it seems that it was flagging again, and it was apparent to many people that if the market was to survive it had to be able to compete with Barrow and Ulverston, both of which by this time had indoor covered markets. The idea that Dalton also needed a market hall gained almost universal acceptance, and with this objective, a petition signed by many leading townspeople was presented to the Local Board.

Once the Local Board had agreed that a market hall should be built, the next question was, where? This soon became an issue of major local importance, and a great deal of controversy raged in the town. The two principal sites considered were Tudor Square, which would have cost about £1,350 to acquire, and Station Road, on land which the Local Board had previously acquired for about 5s. 0d. a yard. For the same area this represents about one-third of the asking price of the Tudor Square site.

A MARKET IN A MIDDENSTEAD.

Tune—A PARSON IN THE PULPIT.

A Market in a middenstead, our town will never suit,
Who'd go to such a Market to buy their fish and fruit ;
Their nose in such a Market most certainly would fail
In its efforts to distinguish the fresh from the stale.

Long life to Capt. Ashburner, J. Askew, and T. Green,
They have been loyal to our town as well as to the Queen.

A Market in a middenstead, selected by our Board,
The wishes of the people are utterly ignored ;
Our Board has turned traitors, the wheat is chok'd with
tares,
Serve them like the Parson that could not say his prayers.

A Market in a middenstead, we must not, will not have,
Though disappointed " dodgers " may shout and howl and
rave,
And flaunt their Acts of Parliament, and secretly combine,
And paint their nasal organs with Perry's choicest wine.

A Market in a middenstead, a going, going, gone,
Record your votes against it, make sure to see it done ;
Then choose yourselves a Market, and choose yourselves a
Board,
That will not see your wishes bamboozled and ignored.

O Yes ! O Yes !

Three groans for Capt. Ashburner, J. Askew
and T. Green,
They are not loyal to our Town as well as to
the Queen.

Ratepayers and Householders of Dalton

Vote for a Covered Market

And do not be kept back by men who oppose on
frivolous, idiotic, and interested grounds.

Must you suffer because the Board have not
chosen the property of the mother-in-law ?

Will you be led by the nose by such a combination
as the three " Who are loyal to our Town as well as to
our Queen," backed by Squills Brobdingnagian, Squills
Liliputian, and Whittle Springs ?

Townsmen, it is not a question of site ! YOU MUST
DECIDE WHETHER YOU HAVE A MARKET HOUSE OR NOT ;
and afterwards, if you object to the site chosen by the
Board, you can effectively oppose the same either by
petition or by appearing at the enquiry, which will be
held by the Local Government Inspector.

Townsmen, Vote FOR a Market, do not be guided
by men who by their action deprived us of Water and
Gas, and would now prevent us from having a Market
House.

21 and 22. Leaflets issued during the 1881 campaign for a covered market.

**23. The proposed new market hall for Dalton. From the supplement to the
Dalton News, 4 November 1882.**

It may have been the case that the man in the street did not mind all that much where the market hall should be situated, but the flames of dissension were fanned by several property owners, and other interested parties who had a vested financial interest in the matter. It is not in the least surprising therefore, that in certain quarters, feelings ran high, reputations were tarnished and the integrity of the various protagonists was questioned.

The issue was finally resolved when in January 1882 the Local Board resolved to erect a market house and offices in Station Road. Designs were chosen, and sanction for a loan obtained from the Local Government Board in March 1883, but, the following month, the original idea of erecting a market house was scrapped, and the Board eventually erected offices, a fire station and stables on the site. It may be that the Board's decision not to erect a market hall was a major contributory factor in the decline and eventual demise of Dalton's ancient market. However, in 1981, exactly one century after the market house campaign, the Dalton and District Civic Society successfully applied to the Barrow-in-Furness Borough Council for permission to re-establish the Dalton market. It was eventually reopened on 7 December 1982.

Social Problems

Apart from the 'hospital' at Bow Bridge which could obviously only accommodate a small number of poor people, we have no knowledge of any other home for the destitute in the parish of Dalton until the workhouse at Billincoat was opened in 1735. The first page of the account book is inscribed 'The workhouse for Dalton Opened June 11th 1735 By Mr. Hinde To serve ye poore & Blinde'. On the next page, the names of the 'Directors for the poore house of Dalton' for that year are given as 'Mr. Tho: Atkinson, Mr. Rich: Postlethwaite, Mr. Wm: Matson, Mr. Tho: Richardson, Mr. Wm: Berry, Mr. Fran: Barker, Mr. John Shaw, [and] Mr. Tho: Bankes'.

From a notebook in the Gaythorpe Collection in Barrow Library (Ref. Z2501), which contains a transcript of the Dalton Workhouse Accounts, we learn that Mr. Hinde's quarterly 'sallary for managing the poor-house' was £1 5s. From the same source we have 'a tabulated account of those who came into the workhouse, the time when they came in, their age, a schedule of their household goods, and the time when they departed the house by death or otherwise is given. The first entry is that of Eliz. Long, aged 80 on 11 June 1735. Her household goods were one iron pot, a tub, a brass pan, a can, a stand, a backboard, 3 pot dishes, 3 wood dishes, a meal barrel, a spiggot pot, a pair of tongs, 2 white handkirchiefs, one blue one white apron, 3 capps, 3 wood boxes, 3 shifts. She died on 5 August, 1735'. This relatively lengthy list of personal possessions, her old age and early death in the workhouse, strongly suggests that Elizabeth Long was removed there from the comparative luxury of her own home either because of illness or senility, or both. Other people, however, were not so fortunate; some had no household possessions at all on admittance to the poorhouse.

Whenever possible, workhouse children were placed in the care of local tradesmen, sometimes in lieu of repayment of a debt as was the case with John Addison
who on 18 May 1741 'agreed to keep & maintain Thomas Park's Child now in the
Workhouse of Dalton sufficiently with meal drink & apparell for two years & to
deliver up the same Child in as good Repair in Clothing as Shee is now Delivered
to him & for payment & satisfaction he the said John Addison to be acquitted of
a debt of five pounds with interest due from him to the parishioners of Dalton . . .'.
The accounts include weekly entries showing food and materials purchased, and
opposite each entry, the weekly amount of yarn spun by the inmates together
with its value. In Christmas week 1740, two additional purchases ('raisings 6d.
shuger 4d.'), suggest that a Christmas pudding had been made. The frequent
mention of 'hops', 'wort dish & barrel' shows that beer must have been brewed
on the premises. There are a number of other interesting entries, such as: 'Bleed-
ing ould Dolly 0. 0. 6d.)'.

For 90 years, until the new workhouse on Goose Green was opened in 1826,
the parish paupers were housed at Billincoat. It is virtually impossible for anyone
living today to visualise just what it must have been like in the workhouse, so long
ago; but some idea of the situation may be gained from the following extract
from an inquiry (now in the Barrow Record Office) into the death of an unfortunate young woman, Mary Simpson, who was forcibly expelled from the Dalton
workhouse because she came from Cumberland, and the parish did not want to
bear the cost of looking after her and her child. Unfortunately, the verdict in this
case is not known, but from the lawyers' comments at the end, it seems likely
that the accused persons would only be fined.

> County of Lancaster. To wit. The Information of Eliz: Askew of Lady Hall, midwife
>   taken upon Oath before me one of his Majestie's Justices of the
>   Peace in and for the sd. County this 25 day of May 1744.
>
> Who saith that on the Monday morning before about two o'clock she was called to assist
> Mary Simpson, who was then in Labour of a Bastard Child at the House of Joseph Har-
> greaves at Lady Hall aforesd. that the said Simpson declared she had Labour pains upon
> her the day before and had been very ill in the Workhouse at Dalton about a fortnight
> before and expected to lie in there and that she was in Greatest Concern and fear when
> she saw the Inhabitants of Dalton come with a Horse and Pillion so as to fetch her away
> and fell into a violent Sweat thereupon and that the Inhabitants of the parish of Dalton
> used threatening words to induce her to come from the sd. Workhouse that James Hall
> who rode before her rode fast and that she was much jumbled and hurt by the riding, and
> this Informant believes that considering the Circumstances she found the said Simpson in
> that she was much Hurt by the riding and brought into a condition thereby which pre-
> vented her Delivery, which she could fully explain to a Midwife or Surgeon and that
> she Died in Labour without being delivered, on the Tuesday morning following.
>
> Sworn before me   Eliz: Askew
> R. G. Sawrey   her Mark
>
>
> According to the forgoing Informations, are the Persons Bailable by one or more Justices
> of the Peace, or ought they to be Comitted. or may the Friends of the Disceased, who
> are Poor, Compound the matter without bringing any Blame upon the Justices who took

the Informations. It had been proper in this case to have had a Coroners Inquest upon ye Body of ye decd., which if it had found ye force us'd to ye dec'd to be ye Cause of her death woud have remov'd ye Doubt as to ye Bailm't as ye Case appears on these Informations, ye woman being dead, & her death probably occasioned by ye Removeall of her or ye violence us'd therein (as may be collected from El. Askew's information) & such Removeall being an illegall act, against ye Consent of ye woman, I apprehend ye offence is such as ye offenders ought not in prudence to be bailed by ye Justices, but they, ye offenders, should be committed & brought to tryall.

Ric. Wilson
June 26, 1744

Its Probable that if the Persons within mention'd should be Indicted for Murder, that they will be acquited: Had they not better be Indicted for a Misdemeanor? or for booth? in two Seperate Indictments, one of the Persons within mention'd was no otherwise than accidentaly in Company when the Woman was sent away, and another was only a Guide over the Sandys; tho' its most likely he knew on what account the Woman was Removed, may not these or one of them be left out of the Committment or admitted as Evidence against the Overseer of the Poor, Churchwarden, & Master of the Work House, who were the Principle Contrivers and Promoters of the Illegal Removal.

The workhouse remained at Billincoat until 1826 when the new workhouse on Goose Green was opened. The average number of paupers housed in the new workhouse was about 35; but it was not destined to last very long for in 1836, upon the establishment of the Ulverston Union under the Poor Law Amendment Act, the Dalton paupers, along with others from this area were transferred to the Ulverston workhouse.

Poverty, as always, caused many problems. It made men lie, cheat and steal when otherwise there would have been no need to. But perhaps one of its most tragic manifestations lay in the fact that in many homes young children were left alone because both parents had to work. In his diary, William Fisher records several instances of unsupervised children being burned or scalded to death. Many of the older children had to work in the fields, sometimes with tragic consequences as can be seen from the following extract from the same diary: 'July 27, 1826: A little girl of Robt Kendals of Barrow having been sent from the shearing field for a piece of fire to light her grandmother's pipe was so dreadfully burned that she died a few Days afterwards it is supposed that she had covered the fire with a part of her dress and in running it had ignited . . .'.

Mr. Fleming, a gentleman farmer from Pennington, sheds more light on the prevailing social conditions at the beginning of the last century in his diary. He is particularly scathing, rightly or wrongly, about the lewd behaviour of the vicar of Dalton, as in this entry made in January 1806: 'Wherever there are poor and idle inhabitants many crimes are committed, and Dalton was no exception. If the clergyman and principal inhabitants be addicted to vice and immorality, the lower classes follow their example and generally exceed them. At Dalton I'm sorry to say the truth of these observations is too evident . . . Good teaching by our betters and clergymen constitute the basis of morality. The pastor has great influence over his flock, but here in Dalton we have the clergyman whose name I forebear to mention, so posterity shall not know such a man was ever entered to

Holy Orders, and so disgrace the gown . . . This pastor was renowned for his drunkenness and lying. Often he was in a shameful state of intoxication as rendered him unable to do his duty . . . Frequently some funeral service is hicupped over in a way that renders it distressing to the auditors. His language is filled with lies, oaths and Immorality . . .'.

In the same entry from his diary, Fleming comments upon the morality of the townspeople, particularly the children, at the time William Close was establishing his practice as a surgeon and apothecary in Dalton: 'He [Close] noted the ignorance and dissolute behaviour of the local children, for which their parents were responsible, their own ignorance and despondency being carried to their children. To remedy this, or even to attempt to stop its further growth Mr. Close attempted to distract some of these children from their idle habits and educate them to use their time usefully, for idleness generates many vices. Much good resulted from the establishment. A reformation of manners was in the main due to the doctor's efforts. The time that used to be spent in idleness and mischief, was now appropriated in usefulness and pleasing amusements . . .'. Just how reliable Fleming's comments are is questionable, for criticism of others is by no means uncommon in his writings. Earlier in this particular account, in a brief biography of William Close he has been unjustly critical of his education and intelligence. Perhaps the following description of Close is nearer the truth.

'This remarkable person was born at Field Broughton in the parish of Cartmel on or about 25 May 1775. While he was still a young child, he went with his parents to live at Walney, which at that time was in the parish of Dalton. It was here that William grew up and went to school where he was taught by the Rev. Samuel Hunter, the curate-schoolmaster of Walney Island. Surrounded as he was by the sea, it is not in the least surprising that one of William's earliest ambitions was to become a sailor; but his parents had other ideas about his future career, and in 1790 he became apprenticed to Mr. Roger Parkinson, a surgeon, at Burton-in-Kendal. From Burton he moved to Edinburgh, where he studied at the University, obtaining his diploma on 18 April 1797. Now a qualifed surgeon, he moved to Dalton and established his practice there on 12 May 1797.'

One would have assumed that the inevitably busy life of a country doctor would leave little time for other interests; but, in William Close's case nothing could be further from the truth. He was also an artist, writer, local historian, musician and inventor. Among his drawings which have survived are sketches of the castles at Dalton, Gleaston and Piel, which with a number of others, are all included in the 86-page supplement which he wrote and included in his own revised edition of West's *Antiquities of Furness*.

In 1803, he married Miss Isabel Charnock at Dalton Parish Church. They lived at No. 2, Castle Street, where their two children were born. John was born in 1805, and their daughter Jane in November 1806. Jane Close died in 1866 while still living in the same house in Castle Street, and was long remembered for her kindly acts, especially in visiting and attending to the sick.

On Sunday 27 June 1813, after having suffered from consumption for some considerable time, William Close died. He was only 38. On the Tuesday following his death, he was buried at Walney under an ash tree in the north-west corner of the chapel burial ground, having been borne there, as was then the custom, by eight men, each of whom was presented with a pair of high-legged boots. By his own request, his grave was nine feet deep, and no memorial stone ever marked the place.

Perhaps, however, the following extract from an anonymous manuscript, obviously written by someone who knew William Close well, could form a fitting epitaph:

On Sunday the 27th day of June 1813 in the 39th year of his age Mr. William Close of Dalton in Furness, Surgeon and apothecary . . . His death was most deeply lamented by all to whom he was known, but most especially by the Inhabitants of Furness, who highly and deservedly esteemed him for his diligent attention to the duties of his profession, in the successful discharge of which he proved himself an intelligent Practitioner — In his attendance on the sick he was delicate and tender hearted, and always ready, without recompence, to give assistance to the poor — No Man ever excelled him in the Virtues of Candour, Sincerity and Benevolence. Amidst the toils and daily Labours on his profession, he wrote and published several essays of great Merit on Subjects of Philosophy and the Arts — In his papers inserted in Nicholson's Philosophical Journal he details in elegant and perspicuous Language, the particulars of many Inventions and Discoveries, which display Talents and Originality of Thought truly wonderful — truly wonderful, when it is considered, that all the learning he derived from education, was acquired before he was ten years of Age, and that Lilly's Grammar was the highest Book taught him at School . . .

In Dalton, much to the regret of many of the more respectable members of the community, the practice developed of hiring farm workers on Sundays during harvest time. Farmers and reapers from far and wide used to congregate in the town and this resulted in drunkenness and rowdy, disorderly behaviour which lasted from Saturday night until Monday morning. A contributor to the *Westmorland Gazette* gives the following description: 'Picture', says he, 'to yourself some three or four hundred men, some sober, some partially and others wholly drunk, sitting, standing, cursing, reviling and committing all manner of abomination, and here and there a sickle merchant and apple woman vending their respective wares in the narrow part of a long straggling town directly between two of Satan's temples, into and out of which the passage is incessant and the crowd so dense, that if you have the ill-fortune of being obliged to go through it, a considerable quantity of muscular power must be spent to effect that object, and if effected without insult, congratulate yourself on being so favoured; altogether it is one of the wildest and most disgraceful scenes of riot, confusion, brutality and drunkenness which can well be imagined'.

In an attempt to restrain this riotous conduct it was decided that a lock-up should be built, and on 6 August 1828, the Four and Twenty ordered that such a building should be immediately built in the workhouse yard. It was about 1840 when the Sunday hirings ceased at Dalton, but the lock-up continued to be used for some time after this.

Soulby's *Ulverston Advertiser* on 19 October 1848 contained the following description of the lock-up: 'Dalton Lock-up House. (Inspected October 8, 1847).

This lock-up house consists of a single cell, about 7 feet long, 6 feet wide, and 10 feet high. It stands outside the village, in an inconvenient and low situation. In winter the cell is damp. There is no provision either for lighting or warming it, but there is a hole for the admission of air. There is a wooden guard-bed, with loose straw for bedding. The place is quite insecure. There is no accommodation for a resident keeper. The cell was in a disorderly condition. The constable stated that the lock-up house was seldom used; that there had been no one in it for a month; and that, in winter, he never kept a person in during the night. The constable had a respectable appearance'.

In the latter part of the century when the Whit Tuesday procession became a popular event, another group of disreputable characters appeared on the scene. Today, nothing would be known about this group of men who called themselves the Slonk Club, were it not for the fact that by their idiotic and disgraceful behaviour in the Whit Tuesday processions they asked for, and received, a good deal of adverse comment in the local press. The following account, taken from the *Dalton News*, 7 June 1884, gives some idea of their activities:

> The usual Whitsuntide parade of 'Dalton Slonks', as they delight to call themselves, took place yesterday. Every year there are a lot of thirsty individuals, lost to all sense of shame, or without one spark of manliness, who band themselves together for no other purpose than getting as much drink as they can and as cheap as they can ... these men carry their cravings for drink to the brink of idiocy, and dress themselves up with ale and porter labels, brushes, and brush sticks ... Yesterday about 30 of these fellows ... assembled at the Bull Hotel, and, headed by a German band, marched on their thirsty errand, calling at each public house for something to drink. It is gratifying that they met with more kicks than halfpence, nevertheless some of them contrived to get intoxicated. The police were on the look-out for them, and came up with them near the castle. Mr. Inspector Smith and Sergent Jump kept a careful watch upon the 'slonks', and followed them into every public house. The slonks entered the Ship Inn, Cavendish, King's Arms, Red Lion, White Horse, but they got nothing, as the presence of the police terrified them from asking for anything. They proceeded to the Nelson Inn, but got no further than the lobby door, as the leader appeared to be terrified at the presence of a policeman ever at his elbow. He hastily came to the conclusion that 'discretion was the better part of valour', and, calling on his men, said, 'I order you to dismiss; all except the band, and I order them to play "God Save the Queen"'.

Eventually, opposition from the public, the police and the local press had the desired effect, and, after a good deal of verbal conflict between various members of the Slonk Club and representatives of the fore-mentioned bodies, the Slonk Club finally ceased to exist in 1885.

In 1841, law and order was maintained in Dalton by a single constable, P.C. William Robinson. Where the constable's office or residence was situated at this time cannot now be determined; but it is reasonable to assume that it was quite close to the lock-up, probably on Goose Green. After the lock-up had closed down, it is almost certain that the next place to be used for the detention of prisoners was a stone building, which can be seen today close to the ginnel behind Beddall's newspaper shop. Presumably this would be about 1850, and it may be that the police station was situated in Market Street, quite close to the new cell.

Within a few years from this date, the police station was situated in what is now a private house, at the junction of Nelson Street and Chapel Street. In 1876, John Smith was the sergeant resident at the police station in Nelson Street. By 1882 he had been promoted to the rank of inspector and had moved to a house in Chapel Street; his place at the police station was taken by Sergeant Isaac Hellam. It may be that these two, assisted no doubt by at least one constable, were so efficient that because of their presence in the town, in November of that year the *Dalton News* could boast 'fortunately for Dalton, there has been a marked absence of crime of all sorts'. A rather remarkable claim for a busy mining town. The elegant new police station in Market Street was opened in 1897 and continued in use until 1968, when the modern new police station situated close to the cenotaph in Station Road was opened.

A magistrates' court was opened in August 1883, to ease the pressure on the Ulverston court, and it was constituted as being suitable for disposing of cases which could be dealt with by one magistrate. In its early days, the Justices of the Peace available for this duty were Mr. E. Wadham, Mr. C. Kirkbride and Colonel Baldwin.

As may be expected in a mining town, there were many cases of drunkenness, wife-beating, gambling etc., brought before the court; but of course, many other crimes were dealt with too. For example the *Dalton News* reported on 20 May 1899 that 'a tramp named James Royle was sentenced to 14 days imprisonment at Lancaster for sleeping out in a barn belonging to Mr. James Atkinson on Sunday night'. The following case, which was tried on 29 April 1899, was reported in the *Dalton News* of that date: 'At Dalton on Saturday before Mr. Ed. Wadham, Phyllis Smith, a tramping hawker was charged in custody with telling fortunes to Miss E. Jones of Dalton, in order to impose on her. Miss Jones stated that the prisoner called at her house in Nelson Street, and offered for sale a quantity of lace, of which she bought to the value of 1s. 6d. After she had bought this, the accused then promised to tell her fortune. For this she offered her three-pence and sixpence, but the prisoner refused and asked for 2s. 0d., and eventually she gave her that amount. She then asked her to place the coin on her hand, and after making several crosses upon it the prisoner "breathed" on the complainant's hand, and asked her to wish three times. After going through this performance, she asked for another sixpence, and added that if she did not give it to her she would have bad luck for seven years and a day, but if she gave it to her she would have a sovereign for it the same evening. The amount was forfeited, and the prisoner again asked her to wish three times, and consequently she left the house . . . Mr. Wadham, in delivering sentence said it was a serious offence, and he was afraid it was not the first time she had carried on the practice. He did not intend dealing harshly with her, and fined her 2s. 6d. and costs or seven days in default. (A voice from the Court: "Thank you sir, thank you") . . . He considered the complainant should have more sense than to listen to her'.

The last case to be heard in the Dalton court was for a betting offence, when the magistrate was Mr. James Price. This was on 31 October 1928, and marked the end of judicial courts in Dalton.

Leisure and Pleasure

Until the middle of the 19th century Dalton was just a small country town, and it would have been surprising indeed if country sports had not figured prominently in the leisure pursuits of its inhabitants. In this context mention must be made of the Dalton Hunt which began sometime in the 17th century and developed into an event of major local importance, being attended by members of the nobility and gentry from far and wide. At the beginning of the 18th century it was known as the Dalton Route, and consisted of fox hunting during the day, followed by an elegant ball in the evening. A quaint but perhaps rather repulsive ritual formed a traditional part of the evening's festivities — the recently severed head of the fox was dipped into the bowl of punch and stirred round once or twice before anyone partook of it. For some reason now unknown it was discontinued at Dalton in the middle of the 18th century and transferred to Ulverston. This change apparently did not last very long; it received an indifferent reception at Ulverston and was duly brought back to Dalton, where it survived until the year 1789. This description of the Hunt is taken from Baines's *Lancashire*. 'The country is peculiarly adapted to the sports of the field, and till of late years there was an annual festival called the Dalton Hunt, in which the gentlemen of the district partook of this favourite diversion by day, and joined the ladies in the ball-room at night. A suite of rooms was erected in the town and handsomely fitted up for this annual jubilee, which existed as early as the year 1703, as appears from the columns of the *London Gazette*, in which it is styled the Dalton Route, and the pen of an elegant contributor to the *Tatler* has imparted to it additional celebrity. To the regret of the Beaux and Belles of the neighbourhood, the Route was discontinued in the year 1789, and has never since been revived'.

The above-mentioned reference to the article in the *London Gazette* is not accurate. The actual advertisement which appeared in the issue dated August 23–26, 1703, was worded as follows: 'The Yearly Fox and Hare Hunting, famous by the Name of the Dalton Rant [*sic*], discontinued for some years, is, by the Gentlemen of the Counties of Lancaster, Cumberland, and Westmorland, agreed to be revived, and begin at Dalton in Furneis on Monday the 25th of October, to continue for 10 days'.

While some people derived pleasure from killing hares and foxes, others used their leisure moments in a more creative way. Young George Romney, who was destined to become Dalton's most famous son, devoted much of his spare time to science, music and literature; but it was his natural talent for drawing and painting that was ultimately to bring him worldwide recognition as the last of the fashionable 18th-century portrait painters. He was born at Beckside, Dalton, on 15 December 1734, one of a family of 10 sons and one daughter, of which all the sons died before reaching middle-age with the exception of George and James, who eventually became a lieutenant-colonel in the Honourable East India Company's Service.

As a boy, George was sent along with his brother, William, to a school at the nearby village of Dendron, where the master, the Rev. Mr. Fell, agreed to teach him the humanities for 5s. 0d. a quarter. He was not a good scholar however, and preferred to spend his time copying, and colouring in crayons the pictures and drawings taken from periodicals and books. When he was 11, he left school and went to work for his father who now lived in a cottage at High Cocken, which he had purchased in 1742 and was situated in another part of the parish of Dalton. George remained here for 10 years, helping his father in his business. Not a lot is known about George's life at this time, but it was in this period that indications of his artistic abilities started to emerge. This fact was commented upon by the dramatist, Richard Cumberland, writing about Romney in the *European Magazine* in June 1803:

> When Mr. Romney has been asked how he first conceived the ambition of becoming a painter, when he had never had the opportunity to contemplate the picture of anything in creation beyond that of the *Red Lion* at Dalton; he explained himself by ascribing his impulses to the opportunities that were thrown in his way by the favour of a labouring man who assisted his father in his husbandry. This labourer being a person of more than common curiosity, put himself to the expense of taking in a monthly Magazine; which besides all the treasures of information and amusement which its miscellanies contained, was enriched with prints, explanatory of the topics that were handled in the work. When the owner had gratified his curiosity, it was his custom to lend his Magazine to his friend George, who neglecting all baser matters, fell to copying the engravings . . .

For a period at least, much of his leisure time was spent in the company of a man called Williamson who lived in Dalton. Williamson, a watchmaker by trade, and 'the general sage and universal referee of the village', had a profound effect on Romney. He taught him to play the violin, and introduced him to the use of the camera obscura. Possibly the greatest influence on the impressionable young Romney was Williamson's interest in alchemy. According to an anonymous author writing in *George Romney*, an undated booklet published by Waddingtons, 'Young Romney was this man's almost constant companion; with him he fiddled, planned, drew, and moreover dipped into the mysterious science of the transmutation of metals. Nor were they idle dreamers, who only sat and amused themselves with strange imaginings; they had a furnace and crucibles, if not all the apparatus with which tradition or history sets up the alchemist. Time, labour, and money were expended in such pursuits, and preparations were made for one grand and crowning experiment which was expected to end in a shower of gold. As the hour drew nigh, the anxiety of the alchemist increased; the fire which had been kept burning for nine months showed flame of a promising colour -- the contents of the crucibles assumed a yellowish hue — and the projector saw in imagination riches rivalling the dreams of Sir Epicure Mammon. It seems his wife, on that fated day, was entertaining a select coterie of gossips, and knowing that workers in fire loved to taste the cup, summoned her husband to make merry. Romney in relating the story, said: "Now Williamson in vain represented that the moment of fate was at hand; his wife's entreaties or remonstrances prevailed; and as he took his seat and drank, his furnace, with all that it contained, blew up"'. The effect of this disaster upon Williamson may well be imagined. His rage and anger knew no bounds, and he blamed his interfering wife for the utter and complete ruination of his life's greatest ambition. He refused to be consoled, and left his home and his wife and finished up living with another woman.

There can be no doubt that his association with Williamson had a deep and profound effect on Romney, for his memories of these, and other happy events from his youth lingered long in his memory. In his later years, when he had achieved almost every ambition he had ever possessed, he remembered Williamson's tragedy and determined to paint a series of pictures depicting the various stages of an alchemist's work, ending, as it did with his friend, in a violent explosion. Unfortunately, this ambition never materialised beyond the stage of a few tentative sketches.

Romney's talents might never have been realised had it not been for a certain Mrs. Gardner of Kendal, who was greatly impressed by some specimens of his work which she saw while visiting his father's house. She suggested that he should do a drawing of her, which he did, and which was probably his first attempt at portraiture. The comments of this lady, and from other people, helped in persuading his father to have George apprenticed to a painter called Steele who was then living at Kendal. The indenture was duly completed and signed, and George began his professional training, which according to the terms of the contract was to last for a period of four years, but which, in fact, was terminated sooner than this because he was reluctant to accompany his master to Ireland.

While living at Kendal, he had married a young lady called Mary Abbot, and this is one reason why he did not wish to accompany Steele on his travels. It soon became obvious to him, however, that if he was to progress further in his career, travel he must, and London was the obvious choice. So on 14 March 1762, he bade farewell to his wife, gave her £30, and, accompanied by two other gentlemen from Kendal he started out on horseback for London, arriving there on 21 March. Although Romney contended that by moving to London he would be better able to support his wife and two young children, this desertion of his family represents a serious blemish in the character of the artist. Even the death of his daughter at the age of three, about a year after he left Kendal, failed to persuade him to return to his wife. In fact, during the whole of his sojourn in London, Paris and Rome, a period of 37 years, he paid only two brief visits to his faithful and devoted wife.

It is well known that during this period he acquired wealth and fame; but, as he grew older, his mental and physical condition started to deteriorate. In the summer of 1799, broken in body and spirit, he left his home and studio at Hampstead and took the Northern coach for Kendal. His wife, as loving and affectionate as ever, received him into her home and tenderly nursed him during the last few months of his life. His brother, Colonel Romney, arrived from the East Indies to see George, and found him so weakened in body and mind that the artist could barely remember him. 'Brother', said Colonel Romney, 'do you not know me?' Romney looked into his face, and burst into an agony of tears. He spoke a few words of recognition, and then forever forgot him and all else that he loved in the world. He then sunk into a state of hopeless imbecility, which lasted without pain or consciousness until 15 November 1802, when he quietly passed away.

His son John decided that his father ought to be buried with his ancestors at Dalton, and that a monument should be erected to his memory in Dalton parish church. When it was finished, the monument was taken to Dalton, but Lord George Cavendish, the lay-rector, refused to allow it to be erected in the church and it was eventually taken back to Kendal and placed in the church there. For many years, his grave stood in a dilapidated and neglected condition in Dalton churchyard, but now, as part of the building programme for the extension to the church, it has been restored to something like its former state of respectability.

*   *   *

On Saturday 12 May 1764, 17 men of Dalton and district met in the house of Thomas Taylor, at the sign of *The White Horse*, and drew up 'the Rules and Directions concerning Dalton's Club' which was, and later became known as 'Dalton Book Club', the members of which have met every month since that date over the past 220 years. There were many book clubs founded in this area in the late 18th and early 19th centuries, but so far as is known, Dalton Book Club is the only one still functioning, and is believed to be unique inasmuch as its records have been preserved almost in their entirety.

The 17 rules covered the whole conduct of the Club and the members signed their names to a declaration that they would form the Club for a period of one year and observe the rules. It follows then that in May each year the Club comes to an end, and it then re-forms at each annual meeting for a further period of one year. In the year 1764 27 books were purchased at a cost of £4 8s. 6d. plus a 'Catalogue of Books for 60 years past' which cost a further 6d. The books consisted of lives of prominent people, travels, and the *Annual Register* for 1763. The secretary kept a register which contained much information of great interest to the present-day historian. In addition to the list of books purchased there was a page listing the names of the members, and against each name was recorded, month by month, a note of the books issued to them. This practice still continues. Then on the following page is a list of the fines levied during the year, and finally particulars of the sale by auction of the books and the prices realised. In the early days the whole of the books were sold at the end of the Club year, and then a new batch was purchased. Nowadays about 30 books are auctioned off each half year and about 80 or 90 books are always available for borrowing.

In the early years most of the fines were as a result of members not bringing in their books but many fines were imposed on members for ill-using books, such as '. . . writing on the fly-leaf (2d.), dropping a sort of red dirt in several places (6d.) and drops of soot at the edge of the leaves (2d.) . . .'. The fines were added to the amount realised by the sale of books, and this paid for the drinks of the members, 8d. being an average price in those days for one gallon of ale. The books purchased during the latter part of the 18th century consisted of essays, memoirs, travels, poetry, histories and sermons, and each year the *Annual Register* was purchased. There were very few novels and to judge from the titles the books made pretty heavy reading. Between 1764 and 1778 the yearly number of books purchased varied between 27 and 45 but by 1800 up to 100 books a year were being bought.

The last 100 years have seen the era of the modern novel and the prolific novelist. The books now offered to the members consist of about half and half novels and a miscellany of what the libraries term 'non-fiction'. Because of the steep increase in the price of hardback books we now include an increasing proportion of paperbacks. The records of members, books issued and other information have throughout the years been kept in registers, each of which has lasted about twenty years. One register covering the period 1898 to 1921 is missing, but all the others have been preserved and are kept in safe custody in the bank. The current register not only contains the present business of the Club but also an alphabetical record of all known past and present members, so far as the missing 1898-1921 register will permit. From 1764 to 1898 there had been 340 members, by 1921 the number was estimated at 375 and the total to day, including present members, is 467.

During the whole life of the Club, meetings have been held in licensed premises. From the inception of the Club, meetings were held in *The White Horse*, and about 1804 the venue was changed to the *Cavendish Arms*. In 1897 a move was made to the *Wellington*, and in 1950 to the Conservative Club. In 1977 the venue was changed to the *Railway Hotel*. Originally the meetings were held on the second Saturday in the month (Saturday being market day), but meetings are now held on the fourth Wednesday in the month. On Wednesday 22 June 1983, the meeting place was changed once again, and the Club now meets in the *Green Goose* Guest House.

*   *   *

Before it was made illegal in 1835, cockfighting was a popular diversion for many, and there were two cockpits in Dalton at the beginning of the 19th century. One of them was in the vicar's garden, which today may seem rather strange, but was not so in those days when it was quite common for the clergy to indulge in this particular pastime. The other one is shown on Merryweather's Map at the foot of Dovecote Lane (Cemetery Hill). Although nothing is now known about what went on in the early days of cockfighting in Dalton, we do have some knowledge of the rules adopted more recently. This information was discovered among some old papers belonging to Mr. W. Massicks of Dalton, who died about 1930, and consists of a set of rules for the conduct of a main, and a model agreement between the contending parties. This information is believed to be unique.

> The laws of fighting put shortly, are as follows: The setters having put down cocks six feet apart, kept back and were not allowed to take up their bird, unless one cock were fast in the other or in the pit or hung in himself, in which case they might be handled and brought to the centre of the pit. If the bird was thrown on his back, it was lawful to turn him over only, but removing feathers from the back or eyes was not generally allowed. If from blindness or any cause the cocks cease to fight the law is told, that is, twice twenty is counted when they are handled and set again. This telling the law is

repeated as long as both cocks fight, but ten only is counted at each interval after they have been put together. Either ceasing to peck is 'told' by a person counting twice twenty. They are then breasted, beak to beak, and if he still refuses ten is counted, announced, and so on loses. This is the 'long law'. Should both be disabled and refuse to fight before the long law begins, it is a drawn battle. Should both refuse fighting during the counting the winner is the cock which fought last. But should he die before the counting is finished, he loses the battle, notwithstanding the other did not fight within the law. The short law is told by a person counting audibly twice twenty and afterwards asking three times: 'Will anyone take it?' If no one accepts the cock is beaten. If, however, it is desired to stop the counting out, the cock may be in the language of the pit, grounded, when he must fight till death, and sometimes unexpectedly recovers and wins.

* * *

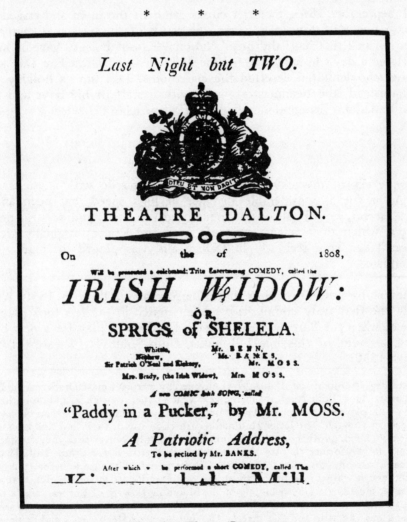

24. Dalton Theatre Programme.

From time to time Dalton was visited by various groups of touring entertainers
— theatre, circuses, fairs etc. In William Fleming's diary for Tuesday 14 October
1806 we find: 'A company of Players at the *White Horse Inn*, Dalton, consisting of 7 or 8 performers, the theatre a hay loft over the stable and the
price of tickets for admittance Pit One Shilling, Gallery 6d.' This appears to
be the earliest reference to theatre at Dalton. There was another theatrical
performance in 1808, when the play 'The Irish Widow' was presented in the
'Theatre Dalton' — quite possibly the same hayloft. Later, the Co-operative
Hall was used almost exclusively for all kinds of dramatic and musical
performances.

On 1 September 1865, Sanger's circus came to the town and staged a grand
procession one mile long. One surprising result of this was that many schoolchildren fell sick that day: the Boys' National School at least, gave up in despair
and declared a day's holiday. On 6 June 1871, it was Dalton Fair Day and once
again the schoolchildren deserted the classrooms. This time a holiday was not
allowed, instead, the headmaster 'went with a staff of big boys and teachers
and captured about fifty and marched them off to school'.

*   *   *

The simple act of thwacking a ball or similar missile with a stick and thus
projecting it for a considerable distance at high speed, has been an eternal
source of secret, boyish pleasure for many grown men, and was no doubt the
seed from which the ancient game of 'Spell and Knurr' originally grew. This
game was taken very seriously in Dalton and was played for many years on
Storey Square.

Cricket clubs were formed in both Barrow and Dalton in 1850. What was
probably the first truly competitive cricket match in Furness took place in the
same year, when the Barrow club challenged Dalton to play for a new ball. The
following account of this match is taken from Soulby's *Ulverston Advertiser*,
22 August 1850:

> On Saturday afternoon last, Dalton was enlivened by a cricket match between the Dalton
> and Barrow clubs. Both clubs are in the first year of their existence, and more than two
> thirds of the players never handled a bat before this year, and not more than two or three
> were ever in a match. The latter club made such good use of their time and ground, and
> attained so much proficiency in this noble and manly game, that they forwarded a
> challenge to the former to play them on their own ground for a new ball. That very
> respectable person, 'the oldest inhabitant' never heard of the game before the present
> summer, and it was so new to the generality of the residents in the district, that a large
> concourse, including a fair sprinkling of the blooming flowers of Furness, was attracted
> to the ground (a large meadow at Crooklands, adjoining the railway), as much to see what
> the game was like as to see that match. The umpires were Messrs. Park and Poole, whose
> decisions gave universal satisfaction. The scrorers Messrs. Matthews and T. Butler. The
> wickets were pitched at two o'clock, and Barrow having won the toss, sent their oppo-
> nents in. The score was as follows:

DALTON

1st Innings			2nd Innings	
Fearon	b. J. Wilson	10	b. J. Wilson	0
Cross	b. Brighton	12	b. Wilson	8
Boulton	b. J. Wilson	8	b. Wilson	0
Butler	b. Brighton	0	b. Brighton	5
Slee	b. J. Wilson	2	b. Brighton	4
Slater	b. Brighton	1	l.b.w.	16
Davis jnr.	not out	3	c. and b. J. Wilson	5
Whiteside	c. J. Wilson b. Brighton	0	not out	3
Fox	b. Arlson	0	b. Brighton	2
Ashburner	b. Brighton	1	c. Ordley b. Postlethwaite	3
Fenton	stumped out	3	c. and b. J. Wilson	0
	Wide	1	Byes	2
		41		48

BARROW

1st Innings			2nd Innings	
Kendall	b. Butler	0	c. and b. Butler	22
Bolton	b. Butler	2	c. Butler b. Cross	1
Wilson (J.)	b. Cross	1	b. Cross	4
Ordley	b. Cross	8	b. Cross	3
Brighton	c. and b. Butler	0	c. Cross b. Butler	1
Postlethwaite	b. Cross	0	b. Butler	0
Wilson (W.)	run out	2	b. Cross	0
Wilson (S.)	c. Butler b. Cross	0	c. Davis b. Cross	0
Huddleston	c. Fenton b. Butler	5	not out	4
Aird	not out	1	c. Cross by Butler	4
	Wide 1; Bye 1	2	Byes	2
		21		41

Dalton consequently winning by 27 runs.

It is interesting to note the low scores and also that this game was apparently played on the ground which was eventually to become the permanent home of cricket in Dalton, although for many years the club experienced great difficulty in obtaining the use of a suitable field and could hardly function at all. By 1883, the club had virtually ceased to exist through lack of a playing field. In October 1884 the *Dalton News* reported that 'At a general meeting last Tuesday, presided over by Mr. G. B. Ashburner, it was decided that a field called 'Hagg's Bottom' be prepared for next year's play. This ground was used many years ago for cricket, is very pleasantly situated, and would doubtless prove a much more attractive ground . . . than any other field in the town . . .'.

In 1891, the club returned to its former ground at Crooklands, and the following year, along with clubs from Barrow, Kendal, Lancaster, Millom, Ulverston and Whitehaven was a founder member of the North Lancashire and District Cricket League. At about the turn of the century however, the club were experiencing severe financial difficulties, and in 1903 it became necessary to cancel all the first team's fixtures. In view of this it seems rather surprising to learn that in April of the same year, they offered to assist in the formation of a tennis club, by laying down four courts to be maintained by the cricket club professional at a cost of £7 10s. for the season. (A lawn tennis club had existed in the town as early as 1890).

Towards the end of the 19th century there were a number of rugby clubs in the town with names like Dalton White Rose, Lillywhites, White Star, Rangers etc. In 1884, a meeting was held in the *Railway Hotel*, presided over by Dr. Patterson, with representatives of all these clubs attending. The object of this meeting was to amalgamate all the smaller clubs into one club which would be known as the Dalton Town Football Club. Although this was unanimously agreed at the meeting, something must have happened to prevent the formation of the new team, for six years later in April 1890, it appears from reports in the *Dalton News* that Dr. Patterson called another meeting for exactly the same purpose. In August 1890, a general meeting of the newly-formed Dalton Town Football Club was held and Mr. R. Todd was elected as captain of the first team, and Mr. G. Calligan as captain of the 'A' team. It was also resolved that the colours of the club be blue jerseys with a red sash over the right shoulder, and white drawers.

Meanwhile, probably about 1885, it seems that another club was formed. This was the Dalton Rugby Football Club; it played in a black and white strip and its home ground was probably Railway Meadow, although it seems certain that a field near Thornton Park, and St Thomas's valley, were also used for matches at different times. About 1905, they abandoned the Rugby Union and became the Dalton Amateur Rugby League Club.

*   *   *

The Dalton Eisteddfods, the first to be held in Furness, were started in 1897 by the Congregationalist minister, the Rev. J. Williams. The programme consisted of competitive solo singing, impromptu speech making, reading at sight an unpunctuated passage, spontaneous answer of questions and an anthem competition for choirs. The following is a selection of some of the questions, with the correct answers, that the competitors in this particular section had to answer in the 1899 Eisteddfod: 'Have you ever seen half a pig's head with two eyes? . . . Yes. With my own two eyes.' 'What noise annoys an oyster most? . . . Any noise annoys an oyster, but a noisy noise annoys an oyster most.' 'Which is easier to spell, fiddle-de-de, or fiddle-de-dum? . . . The former because it is spelt with more ease (e's).' The subject for the impromptu speech was, 'What would you do if you were left with a cross baby?' According to the local press, the efforts of the competitors provided endless amusement. There were twelve entries in the unpunctuated reading competition, part of which read as follows: '. . . in this district I advertised for a wife in the Co-op journal we get some tasty bits my sweetheart has got one eye at the back of his head is a large bump he wears a watch chain under his arm he carries a stick his nose is straight on the top of his head he has a curl we were married in a motor car I rode the other day two horses bolted the other day and fell into a perambulator . . .'.

For several years the Eisteddfod was a great success, always outshining the Ulverston one, which started with great difficulty in 1899. Gradually, however, its popularity declined, probably because no-one could be found to take the place of its founder, who it seems wanted to hand over the responsibility of organising the event to a civic committee.

The period 1870–1910 saw the birth of many clubs, societies, associations etc. in the town. Some of them existed for only a short time, but others flourished and survived for many years. In *The Lake Counties* (by J. D. Marshall and J. K. Walton) it is mentioned that in 1909 there were in Dalton two political clubs, nine sports clubs, and 17 or 18 other clubs. The existence of so many, and such varied activities in such a small town is quite remarkable, and can perhaps be construed as reflecting the overpowering need for leisure activities to contrast with, and relieve the tedium of an otherwise hard life. A list of societies will be found in Appendix Two.

The political clubs referred to were the Conservative Club, which was opened in the presence of a large gathering, on Saturday, 19 March 1887, and the Liberal Club, which opened its premises in Hall Street on 8 January 1897. The latter remained active until about 1947, when the premises were purchased by the Baldwin Masonic Hall Company Ltd. The Conservative Club was originally situated in Station Road, in what is now the Dalton Baths Fund Shop. The opening ceremony was performed by Mr. W. G. Ainslie, M.P., and Mr. Edward Wadham and Mr. Godby were elected as chairman and secretary respectively. In 1914, the club moved to its present premises at the corner of Station Road and Beckside Lane.

By about 1870, the musical scene in Dalton seems to have been rich and varied with an incredible number of bands, orchestras, choirs and minstrel troupes all drawing on the same reservoir of talent. Of the bands in the town at this time, the names alone are worth recording. They included: The Scrap Band, The Volunteer Band, The Flute Band, The Bread and Treacle Band, Park Mines Band and several others. The story of the bands in Dalton at this time is complicated, fascinating, and at times very humourous, and would be an excellent subject for further research. Here we can do no more than give a brief outline.

The constantly changing pattern of the Dalton band scene makes it difficult to pin-point the precise beginning of the Town Band, but it seems to have been about 1870. From newspaper reports and a short anonymous chronicle in the town band's record book, it appears that in 1894, the two principal bands were the town band and the Salvation Army band, and that the Salvation Army band under the able leadership of Bandmaster Jim Coward who later emigrated to South Africa and became Mayor of Germiston in the Transvaal, was the more successful of the two. It included in its ranks several fine musicians; among them were Albert and Herbert Williams, brothers of Sir Thomas Melling-Williams, later according to an undated cutting from the *Dalton News*, of the British Air Command.

In January 1897 the annual meeting of the town band was held at the *Wellington Hotel*, and the following officers were elected: Mr. T. Deason as chairman; Mr. R. Atkinson as treasurer; Mr. W. Boundy as secretary; and Mr. H. Baker as conductor. Very soon after this meeting had taken place, there was some disagreement among the members of the band, and, whatever the cause may have been, it was serious enough to make some of them terminate their association with the town band and start a band of their own. This was officially formed as the Amateur Brass Band at a meeting held in the *Wellington Hotel* in March 1897. Mr. H. Baker was appointed as conductor of the new band which survived for many years, and frequently performed at concerts, parades, etc.

Bob Atkinson remained loyal to the town band, and in the succeeding years established his reputation as a solo euphonium player. His fame spread rapidly, and it was not long before many of the leading bands of Lancashire and Yorkshire started making him tempting offers for his services. A well-known band of the time 'Besses o' th' Barn', almost succeeded in clinching the deal, but they never knew that his final refusal of their offer depended entirely on the toss of a coin.

One result of the difference of opinion between the two factions was that the town band was left in a sadly depleted condition and without a conductor. Fortunately for them, it was only a matter of a few weeks before they acquired the services of Mr. John H. Carter of Roose, a man who was destined to lead the band to a greater glory than they had ever known before – or since. Under his inspired leadership, they entered and won competitions, and became known as the Dalton Town Prize Band. Mr. Carter resigned as conductor on 2 April 1913, and his place was taken by Mr. Atkinson, who because of ill health was unable to join the army when war broke out the following year. This, together with the fact that many of the members of the band were miners, who were exempt from military service and not required to work weekends, meant that during the war years Bob's Band, as it became known, was the only one in Furness that could meet and practise regularly. It was in constant demand to play at concerts, galas, etc., and raised a great deal of money for the war effort and charity.

Religion and Education

Until the year 1823, there were no organised religious services for nonconformists in the town; and there was not even a building where such groups could meet to worship. This was soon destined to change, for the number of people belonging to other denominations was beginning to increase as people came to the town from other parts of the country in search of work. Soon, with the rapid growth of the local mining industry, the trickle was to become a flood; but in the beginning their numbers were small. The opposition they encountered from the established church and its supporters was quite severe. According to one source,[9] the birth of nonconformity in Dalton came about as follows:

> The Wesleyan Methodists had at this time a small meeting house in Ulverston, to which, one Sunday morning in 1823, three earnest Dalton young men were walking, when they

were accosted by a Primitive Methodist missionary, the Rev. F. H. Jersey, who inquired where they were going, and on hearing their answer, asked them to return with him, saying 'I am going to storm Dalton'. They returned. An open-air service was held at the Market Cross that morning and on several subsequent Sundays. Organised opposition of a formidable kind soon showed itself. One morning someone had engaged three men to blow horns close to the ears of the missionary, and a quarrel ensued between these and others who wished to hear the preacher. The result was that a few days later Mr. Jersey was served with a warrant, 'for conducting riotous and tumultous worship at the Market Cross, Dalton', and was by the magistrates committed to Lancaster Castle for four months, but he was afterwards bailed out. On that Sunday morning when Mr. Jersey first visited Dalton he concluded his open-air service before the regular church service began. He was strongly condemned by the clergy, and so reproached were those who had listened to him that they decided to find a separate place of worship of their own. A room was not easily secured, and services were held for some time in a Quarry Hole at the top of Skelgate. At length an 'upper room' was placed at their disposal, which was no other than a hayloft over a stable situated at the foot of Skelgate. In this room in the year 1823 the Wesleyan Methodists established a society and a Sunday School. It is uncertain at what date the chapel was built at the top of Skelgate, but it was occupied as early as 1828. From that time until 1864, it was the only non-conformist place of worship in the town, and the Wesleyans held it with a growing society and Sunday School, which necessitated once during that period, its enlargement. The present chapel in Wellington Street was built in 1864 . . . The first Wesleyan minister resident in the town was the Rev. Ralph Spoor, who came in 1865.

The other churches and chapels built in the 19th century were the Congregationalist, Market Street in 1869; St Margaret's (C. of E.), Ulverston Road (built in 1872 and rebuilt in 1902); the Bible Christians, Broughton Road, in 1873; the Catholic church , Ulverston Road, in 1879; the Primitive Methodists, Chapel Street, in 1883; and in 1885, the Baptists, in Broughton Road.

By the early 1880s the structural condition of the parish church was causing concern. This, together with the general feeling that Dalton's growing importance merited a much finer church, was sufficient to persuade the church authorities that if the necessary funds could be guaranteed, the old church should be demolished and a new one built on the same site. The idea was generally accepted, and a financial appeal received enthusiastic support from many sources including the Duke of Devonshire, K.G., who was to become the largest single contributor to the fund. So in 1883 demolition work commenced on the old church which had served the town for centuries. During the course of this work, the *Dalton News* reported on 1 December 1883 that when the old church was being pulled down, a number of stones bearing ancient markings, believed to be runic symbols,[10] were discovered in the fabric. If indeed they were runes, and not masons' marks, it would tend to strengthen the popular belief in the antiquity of the church at Dalton.

The designers of the new church were Messrs. Paley and Austin of Lancaster, and the result of their work was a fine example of church architecture. The stained glass window at the east end of the building was presented by the Duke of Devonshire, and the west window in the south aisle by Miss Cleator of Thornton House, Dalton. Other gifts included the oak pulpit (from Mr. Wadham of Millwood), and the lectern and brass eagle (from many friends of the late Mr. A. W. O. Roberts, in his memory).

At the beginning of the last century the school accommodation in the town consisted of the Grammar School, reputed to have been built in 1764, the Free School, dating from 1622, and a small number of private academies. Tyson[11] gives a list of masters of the Grammar School and also of the elementary school, which in all probability was the old Free School on Goose Green. The increasing population towards the end of the century necessitated the building of more schools, and four out of a total of five new schools were opened within six years.

The Boys' National School on Goose Green (which replaced the Free School), was opened on 3 November 1862 by Isaac Helliwell, who earlier that year had been appointed headmaster. Thanks to the meticulous entries made in the log books, it is possible to reproduce here the following extracts which give us a fair idea of the living conditions of these times. This first entry is dated 3 November 1862.

> The opinion of some of the Trustees with respect to the deplorable state of degradation and ignorance of the children was soon made manifest. As a proof of this it may be remarked that several instances of the most dirty habits occurred — also spitting on the floor, wiping noses on their jacket sleeves and collars etc., etc. They were exceedingly filthy in their dress and person — hair uncommonly long and uncombed. They had no idea of order or discipline, but were extremely noisy, rude and ignorant.
>   162 present.
>
> *Thursday 27th Nov.* The school began to assume the appearance of order and work. The children were much pleased with their lessons.
>
> *25th Jan. 1864*   There is so much sickness (some contagious) that, by order of the Rev. J. M. Morgan, chloride of lime was procured and the rooms sprinkled with a solution of it.

The Dalton Board Girls' School was opened on 7 January 1878, and there were 66 pupils. Lately it was the Chapel Street Infants' School, and Mrs. B. Craig was the headmistress. A note in the log book written by the Rev. J. M. Morgan in March 1879, tells us that for many years prior to the 1870s there was a great shortage of school accommodation in the town (presumably only the Free School existed after the Grammar School closed), and despite the fact that many parents wanted their children to be educated, there was nowhere for them to go. As a result of this, many of the children who came to attend the Board Schools in the 8-11 age group would have been more suitably placed in an infant school.

The Board School Boys' Department in Broughton Road was opened on 7 January 1878, and its first headmaster was Mr. E. Myers. On the first day 102 pupils enrolled. On the second day this figure rose to 117, and to 134 by the end of the first week. By the end of the second week there were 177 pupils and 200 by 25 January! The Catholic School in Ulverston Road was opened on 2 August 1880, and had 30 scholars attending in the mornings, and 31 in the afternoons. The Nelson Street School was opened in 1884 as a Junior Mixed School. In January 1887, it became a separate boys' and girls' school, and on 9 January 1929, a girls' school only. The following extract from the log books was taken in 1970 by kind permission of Mrs. Smith who was the headmistress at that time: '*Nov. 28 1899*. Walter Davies, although having been warned previously is too familiar with the boys and allows them to take liberties. One boy (McDowell) on being sent out said "Eh! Walter Davies thou's nivver let me off yance — let's off yance". Davies allowed this to pass without rebuke. In telling a boy not to talk he uses such expressions as "Stop your chitter" '.

Chapter Five

TWENTIETH-CENTURY DALTON

The end of the industrial era

AS THE FIRST cold, grey dawn of the 20th century illuminated the sky over Dalton, no-one could dispute the fact that the town was in a state of decline. The graph (below) clearly shows that the production of ore from the Furness iron mines was steadily falling, with the inevitable result that many miners were losing their jobs. This in turn was the reason why almost every week groups of un-employed miners were given a lively but emotional farewell by their friends, relatives, and often at least one brass band, as they boarded the train at Dalton station to seek employment in distant countries.

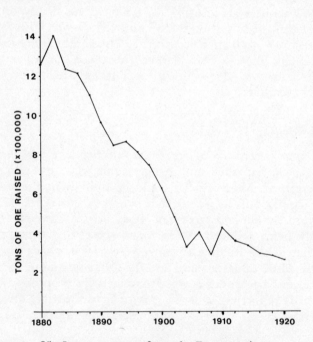

25. Iron ore output from the Furness mines.

The Stainton mines were closed principally as a result of Brogden's bankruptcy in 1884. Longlands, Standing Tarn and Highfield mines were all closed by the beginning of the century through being worked-out or because the cost of pumping water was too high. Yarlside and Stank mines closed down in 1901, followed in 1904 by Harrison, Ainslie mines around Lindal, where high pumping costs, falling yields and poorer quality of ore in depth rendered them unprofitable. Ashburner's mines around Elliscales closed at about the same time. The trouble with the older workings was that the shallow, accessible good quality ore had all been mined first, and as it became necessary to go deeper, the quality of the ore deteriorated and problems with flooding increased. At the beginning of the century, 9,000,000 gallons of water was being pumped daily from the Furness mines, for a corresponding output of less than 200 tons of ore — obviously not a very profitable operation.

Against this picture of pit closures however, the search for new ore deposits continued. The Nigel sop at Roanhead was discovered in 1899, and provided work for many years to come. Dickie Pink's mine was opened at Newton after ore had been discovered there in 1903, and the life of the Park mines was extended for a further few years after scientific prospecting had revealed additional ore deposits. The mines at Lindal were reopened after an injection of capital from London, and a modern power station was built so that the old workings could be drained. At about the same time the mine at Yarlside was reopened to reach ore lying above the natural water level. Anty Cross mine at Dalton was opened about 1916; until 1927 when it was finally drowned-out by an underground stream, it raised both iron and copper ore. The Kennedy mines at Roanhead closed for good in December 1941, closely followed by Yarlside, and in 1944 by Dickie Pink's. This marked the end of an era in the history of Dalton, and it also marked the end of the Furness Miners' and Quarrymen's Union with its 129 members.

Daily life at work and at home

It was inevitable that a century of mining would produce a new breed of men; men who daily faced hardship and danger, and who, by today's standards, expected little in return. Many stories could be told about them and about the often deplorable conditions in which they worked; but much of this valuable information has already slipped from our grasp as the number of surviving ex-miners is gradually being reduced. A few years ago one of them, now deceased, told the author that in the Roanhead mines where he worked, it was considered unlucky to whistle while underground, and for the same reason they would never kill the rats, mice and cockroaches which infested the workings. Perhaps if any single story is worth reporting, even if it is only to illustrate the conditions of employment in those days, it should be the following account of a miner being entombed for a week:

> At this point I would mention the Yarlside slip, that hill-side which can be seen from Furness Abbey and Roose railway station, where a great slice of earth fell away from the hill-side and still leaves bare earth even today. It all happened overnight — one day it was a hill and next morning it was a hole much as it is today. My father was working in

that mine on the night when it happened. I remember him talking about it once when I was a boy. I can't remember the date of the happening [18 January 1915 (Author)] and this little piece of mining history is almost lost like many more of the interesting stories ... However one item did stay with me, it was the way my father described the sinking. The miners knew something was going to happen by the tension and the state of the place; timbers were moving all over the place, and towards the end one could see the props slowly sinking through the floor of the tunnels like matches being pushed into mud very slowly. Word went through the pit for everyone to get out, and it was said at the time that the people in charge were asking the miners to stay and salvage as much of the equipment as possible such as tools, bogies and anything useful, but the miners had had enough and said 'to hell with the equipment, let us get out whilst we can'. It was at Yarlside where a miner by the name of Smiler Park was trapped for seven days before he was dug out; he was in a sorry state when he was saved. He had realised he was to be trapped for some considerable time from the amount of debris behind him, so he gathered together as much materials as he could: a few stubs of candles etc. and sat down to wait. He drank water from the drips from the roof and eventually through hunger ate pieces of candle stubs and chewed his clog uppers. Most of the time he spent in total darkness so he could eat his candle stubs. The story tells of the hard and very harsh conditions of those days because when Smiler Park was released in a terrible state, physically and mentally, he was taken home and cleaned up and then in a day or so he returned to work to find out how he stood with regards to his accident. He went through the routine performance of those days. He respectfully asked at the works offices for permission to see the manager, on being admitted the manager asked, 'Well man, what do you want to see me about?' Smiler suggested could anything be done about some form of compensation for him. At this, the manager exploded, 'Good God man, don't you realise what it cost the firm to dig you out?, go away and consider yourself lucky we took the trouble to save you'. Then Smiler asked what was to be done about his lying time (working time) for the time he was trapped in the pit. The manager said 'Don't talk to me about your lying time, you did no work while you were trapped down there, so don't expect any wages for that part' ...

For many boys leaving school at this time the choice was clear: they either worked as farm labourers, or they went to the mines, usually as metal-pickers. From the same source we have the following story:

I have seen Bill C. (he was the wagon boss at Nigel Pit), go along the wagons to see if his metal-picking lads were at work, and on very cold days these lads would slip away from the pit-head down into the boiler house to warm their frozen fingers on the side of the old Lancashire boilers. It was on one of these occasions that I saw him remove his leather belt and charge into the boiler house. As there was only one entrance to the place, once in they were caught, and the flaying belt created howls as the lads rushed back to their work. Old Bill once remarked that it was better to give them a taste of belt rather than give them the sack ...

Mr. C. adds to the picture: 'I left school when I was thirteen and started work at Roanhead metal picking. Seven shillings a week it was then, fourteen shillings a fortnight — half a gold sovereign and four bob. And you had to be on the road at three o'clock in the morning. Kids wouldn't do that now would they? That's what you had to do. I seen our old lady open the door at two o'clock in the morning and there was two foot of snow — not a foot mark in it, and you had to walk all the way to Roanhead ...

The late Bill Edwards described his boyhood in the mines: 'I remember me and Walt C ... goin' to Park mines lookin' for work. A big Welsh chap was boss over the boys and that. They all had great beards at that time, and we went to him and asked for a job and he said, "There's two boys here today that haven't come, and if they don't come in the morning I'll send 'em back home and you two can start yesterday". Well this puzzled us and after that Walt wouldn't go again, but I went next day and got a job. He was 'aving a bit of fun with us'. Asked to describe his job, Mr. Edwards continued: 'It was what they call pickwheeling. Now my job was to go to the different mines — there was only two anyway, and gather the picks and drills, take 'em up to the blacksmith's shop. After they'd been sharpened an' that, I had to take them back again. For a small kid it was a heavy job because I had to wheel them up like a sort of a ramp, up to where the blacksmith's shop was. And I remember an oldish chap. Oh, he used to shape the wood — there was a name for it. But he used to shape the wood to make the forks. The forks were the stand-up woods down below like, one at each side then one across. They called that the head tree. Well, he said to me when I was coming to the bottom of the hill with the first load, "Tha must rest 'ere for a while" he says, "and once you start goin' don't stop in t' middle or tha'll nivver git goin' again. Tha'll 'ave to unload half of the stuff off". And how right he was. And he says, "now git thy breath before tha starts up there". An' I did, an' I started up this ramp. And you can feel your inside lifting an' that, an' you were gaspin' for breath but you had to keep shovin' away. When I was getting near the top I could feel my eyes popping, you know, comin' out. An' I dropped the things at the top, fell on me arse and me eyes went back. But that was actually what 'appened to me like. I was only thirteen then . . .'.

There can be no doubt that boys and grown men alike found life in the mines very hard, and it has been remarked on more than one occasion that you needed a sense of humour just to keep going; but sometimes even the most stalwart found it difficult to laugh when life seemed to have so little to offer. Things were little better for the wives and mothers at home either. In the 1920s, even in those households where husbands and sons were in employment, their living standards were barely above poverty level. Mrs. Margaret Copley, formerly of Dalton but now living in Lindal, recalled the hardships of her childhood:

There was very little work and poor wages. My father worked at Goldmire quarry . . . in the 1920s he worked there and of course the wages were very poor, and you see they had to work in the rain, if they didn't well there was no money; and it would rain day after day and he'd come home wet through and they used to put sacks round their shoulders, and they'd be wet through, and fasten sacks around their legs, they'd be wet through. I can remember my mother used to cry, because at the end of the week there was hardly anything to pick up after a very wet week. And we lived in Devonshire Street at that time. I was born in Devonshire Street . . . There was awful epidemics of diptheria and scarlet fever, and there was also consumption — we later called it tuberculosis didn't we? But in the old days it was called consumption. Well people just died you know, and High Carley was full, and Oubas House was where the children were and that was full. It was a terrible thing . . . I can remember having scarlet fever, and my brother, we had it at the same time and, oh, it was a terrible illness then, it was really. You know, people died even with that then, but you never hear of it now do you?

Of course there was no electricity then in the twenties. It was oil lamps and candles, and, oh dearie me, great big black cooking stoves. You know, I think back about all the cooking that my mother used to do on the open fire, I don't know how they'd turn such meals out, because I mean, there was nothing else . . . My mother used to boil cabbage and then fry it. We had that many a dinner time. And she used to fry potatoes and onion and she used to call it raw fry . . . We never got meat. The only meat we could afford was perhaps three pennyworth of cuttings to make a hot-pot, and that was on a Sunday, not through the week. You know, my mother used to boil one egg, and I often wonder even now - and I'm sixty two now — I often say to my grandchildren that my mother, she'd boil one egg, and there were three of us then, and she used to dole us out with what we called an egg cake each. I don't know how many rounds of bread we didn't get with egg on. It was all out of one egg. I don't know how she did it . . . Mr. Woodburn he was what they called the relieving officer, and if you were out of work or off sick or anything, you went there and, well they didn't give you money, they gave you a ticket and you could take that to one of the grocery shops and then you could get flour and treacle - that's where he got his name from, Treacle Joe. That was perfectly true. But I mean, he wasn't disrespected or anything like that, don't get me wrong, it was, you know, like a sort of nick-name really, because that's what you got, lard and flour and treacle and possibly margarine. The necessities you see, you got.

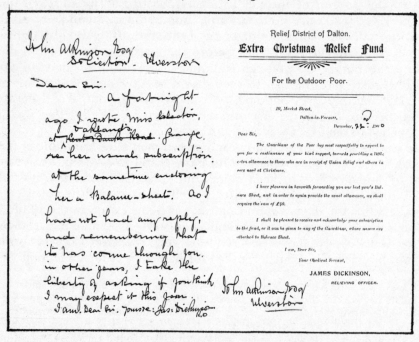

26. Copy of letter from Dalton Receiving Officer requesting the usual
contribution from Miss Cleator.

This grim picture was confirmed by Mr. C., who stated that 'they were only getting eighteen bob a week labouring at the shipyard then. 'Course, food stuff was cheaper, but it was best sheep heads for broth an' all that. They wouldn't eat sheep heads now. Used to go down to the butchers for three penn'orth o' cuttings. They used to have big heaps on t' counter — all freshly cut-off meat. Bits here, bits there, Pig's feet and all sorts. Used to get threepenn'orth to make a pie. Get the old broth pan out wi' a couple o' sheeps heads in it. The old woman used to wrap the brains up in a bit o' muslin and put a bit of cotton round 'em, put 'em in the pan and them was hers. They wouldn't eat brains now would they? When anybody died they used to come round with a book y' see, collecting, threepence or sixpence or whatever you could give. That's how bad it was. This council 'ere ' ad two hearses. One was for them as could pay, and there was one for paupers. One had glass windows in, two little glass doors at the back, paupers' hearse had nowt -- just a wooden box . . if they were a pauper, once over they wouldn't read a burial service over 'em. That's summat isn't it? An old woman in Buccleuch Street died, a woman called W ——. She lied in the house our old lady told me for — a red hot summer it was — for a fortnight. Nobody'd read a burial service over 'er. Finished up with the Salvation Army burying 'er . . .'.

As the economic depression of the 1920s and early '30s continued to bite, unemployment soared, and a number of schemes designed to help the unfortunate victims of the recession were introduced. In 1930, for example, 107 people from Dalton applied for a free issue of seeds, fertilisers, etc. which was being made available by the Coalfields Distress Fund. A temporary employment scheme was also introduced, and this account of his recruitment into it by Bill Edwards is given here as a character study in simple, rustic humour:

Everybody was out of work . . . We had that club up at where the old *King's Arms* was you know. Upstairs. But anyway, they came up there one day, the chap that used to look after it, he said 'any of you chaps want a job for a week?', and I thought that's alright. Two pounds for a week's work. So I said to my mate Nattie, I said 'how about it?', but he wasn't keen at first . . . but we went to this job. It was at Newton. There's a stile there as you're going in on the right hand side, it might still be there, and there was a blasted big boulder, one of those round, polished boulders that runs in veins like, if you will. And we had a big hammer there, and we sat in the hedge arguing who was going to break it up like.

Question. Who was actually employing you?

It was the council . . . they didn't force you, you had to volunteer. And we sat and we were arguing over this 'ere boulder, and I said to Nattie, I said 'you know, it won't be easy to break that. You could knock your wrist up or many a thing'. He said 'well we'll likely have a go at it'. 'Well' I said, 'you start if you want to'. 'No' he said, 'I'm not going to start'. And I said 'well let's sit down and think about it for a while, it's no good rushing into a job like this'. Now Sam ——, he was the charge-hand. Nice chap. He was the charge-hand and we could see him up at the top of the road. He'd took us down there and showed us what we had to do. So we sat, and I said 'let's give it a think'. I said 'we'll go out in the middle of the road and you offer to get hold of me as if tha's going to strike me, and we're supposed to be arguing like hell'. He said 'what's that for?' I said 'Sam'll come down, don't worry. He'll come down and help'. So it happened. He'd spotted us had big Sam, he come down. 'Now me lads, what's up now?' I says 'its this feller here, he's arguing about napping this 'ere boulder up, and I'm telling him it needs an experienced quarry-man to know how the vein runs, and one thing and another, to nap that up, and he's telling me where the hell are we going to find one?' 'Aye', Sam says, 'where?' I says 'well the only one I know is thee'. I told him 'thou could nap it up'. And he did, daft as a brush, and we sat in the dyke and watched him . . .'

Transport

From the beginning of the century, the expansion of the Barrow shipyard and other industries had provided steadily increasing employment for many of the inhabitants of Dalton. By 1914, between five and seven hundred men made their way to Dalton station each morning to catch the 5.20 a.m. train to Barrow. In this same year, the British Electric Tramway Company applied for a licence to operate an omnibus service between Barrow, Dalton and Ulverston. The service commenced in 1915 with three buses running on the route. It cannot have been very profitable however, for almost immediately they offered the undertaking to Barrow Corporation for £15,000, and although the offer was declined at this time, the Corporation did complete the purchase in 1919.

In the early 1920s there were several bus companies in the area. In Dalton a Mr. Quinlan ran a small fleet of buses known locally as Quinneys. These buses were quite small, only six to eight-seaters; they were painted olive green, with a door at the back and two bench seats facing each other inside. Many a local shopkeeper cursed them for taking trade out of the town. Later, there were a number of larger 14-seater buses operating through the town. These vehicles had names painted on their sides; among them were 'Scarlet Runner', 'Silver King', 'Princess' and 'Sportsman'. When running between Barrow and Ulverston, it was commonplace for all the passengers to have to disembark at the foot of steep hills and walk to the top so that the empty bus could then laboriously chug its way up the hill, where the passengers would then board the vehicle and continue their journey. 'Scarlet Runner' ended its days by catching fire at the top of Melton hill and was completely destroyed.

It was about 1930 when the Furness Omnibus Company Ltd. was formed, and established its garage and office in Beckside, Dalton. It was also at about this time that the Barrow Corporation buses — coloured blue and cream — commenced a regular service between Barrow and Ulverston. The Furness Omnibus Company owned and operated 21-seater Leyland Leverettes on country routes all over Furness. Before long, the Grange Motor Company joined the several other companies operating in Furness, among which were the 'Blue Pullman', which were rather luxurious with curtained windows, and the Barrow Bus Company, whose vehicles were painted yellow and brown. Two of the Furness Omnibus Company's vehicles, numbers 13 and 14, were somewhat unusual in that they had small tables between the seats. All the company's buses were painted red and known locally as the 'red buses', a name which persisted well into the earlier days of their takeover of the Ribble Motor Services.

In 1923, the Furness Railway became a constituent of the London, Midland and Scottish Railway, and at first no great changes were apparent. A few years later however, the mid-20s saw the great depression and the closure of a number of local mines, and with them went the Whitrigg and Henning lines. As a result of increasing road competition, passenger traffic also started decreasing with the result that the number of men employed as station staff was drastically reduced. Eventually the local trains to Ulverston, Millom etc. were stopped. Finally, in the 1960s, under British Railways' rule, the Stainton branch line was closed and Dalton station became an unstaffed halt. The canopies were removed from above the platforms, and at the same time the goods yard was closed down.

The increasing use and popularity of the internal combustion engine affected the fire-brigade about 1926, when the old horse-drawn appliance – the 'Duchess of Fife' – was replaced by a small Dennis motor vehicle. This, in turn was replaced in 1934 with a Leyland Cub, which was bought with a £960 loan from the Ministry of Health.

By this time the fire-engine was housed in a single bay appliance room situated in Station Road and forming part of the Town Hall building. Fire calls were received by the boiler-house attendants at the gasworks, and they shared an annual honorarium of £5 for providing this service. In 1948, the gasworks closed down, and the operators at the telephone exchange took over the duties of accepting fire calls. In 1963, a direct telephone line between the station and Divisional Control at Lancaster was established, and from this time all emergency calls were received at Lancaster. In 1972, pocket alerters were issued to all personnel, thus replacing the siren and call bells which had hitherto been used. It was on 4 December 1969 that the brigade transferred to its new headquarters at Butts Beck, although the new station was not officially opened until 4 June 1970. At the present time, the officer-in-charge is Sub-Officer G. F. Hayes.

Leisure

Dalton's traditional October fair survived for over six hundred years – certainly at least until the 1880s. At this time, in fact, there were three annual fairs: the Spring Fair on 28 April, first held in the year 1803, mainly for the showing of cattle and hiring of servants; the Summer Fair on 6 June; and the Autumn Fair which was still held on 23 October. By the beginning of the 20th century, however, the only fair of any note was the Whit Tuesday fair, and there are many people alive today who can remember the stalls spread along the length of Market Street from Tudor Square to the Cross, where traditionally the swing boats were in front of the castle, and a shooting gallery in front of the *Cavendish Arms*. In Station Road, there used to be a moving picture show with sound, hopefully synchronised, provided by a large phonograph of the cylindrical type. An added attraction in Station Road was a noisy, brightly lit steam organ, which entertained the crowds with old favourites such as 'William Tell'.

In those days, Whit Tuesday was quite a gala day in Dalton. The festivities started with the 'Club Walk' which took place in the morning. This was a procession to the parish church organised by various local Friendly Societies and quite a sight it must have been with its banners, tableaux, and young boys on horseback, dressed in green, representing foresters. In the afternoon, there was a gala on the cricket field. The decline of the Whit fair started when the Great War broke out in 1914, and although it was resumed after the war, it never really recovered its former glory. The arrival on the scene of the motor car also contributed to its demise, and it is perhaps to be regretted that Dalton will probably never again see a festival such as this.

In the late 19th and early 20th centuries, most of the live entertainment in the town was provided by the considerable number of societies which existed at that time, from which there issued a constant stream of events, including drama, literary gatherings and musical presentations of many kinds. It is quite obvious from reading contemporary newspapers that there was always something happening, as indeed there had to be in those days before the advent of the cinema and wireless made this particular kind of home-grown entertainment less necessary.

As well as various dramatic and musical presentations, the Co-operative Hall also staged magic lantern slide shows. These, of course, were the forerunner of the moving picture shows — the cinema — which was soon to stagger the imagination of its audiences and transport them for a short time to distant exotic places and weird and wonderful adventures. It is believed that Dalton's first cinema, the Empire, was opened in 1912. It was built in Market Street on the site formerly occupied by the Dalton Brewery, and its proprietors were two gentlemen named Backhouse and Drinkwater who had recently returned to Dalton from South Africa. The Co-operative Hall became a cinema about 1919.

The early days of the cinema in Dalton have been described by a gentleman, who is now a senior citizen. The following is an extract from his account: 'In the 1920 decade and the silent films, Jack Backhouse was the manager, and he tried to keep people happy in the hard times. I remember a seat in the front stalls cost threepence in old money. They were long wooden forms with fold-back seats (no cushions). Then, the back stalls cost fivepence. These were fold-back forms with a fabric covering. Right at the back were the plush seats known as "cosy corner". These seats cost sevenpence. It was on one of those Saturday nights (first house), when the back row of the front stalls was crammed full of very heavy and stout ladies. The lights had just been dimmed and the show started, when suddenly, there was a terrific crash, and all the stout ladies were on the floor and some wedged between the row. The show was stopped and the lights put on — the long form had given way under the weight. Hasty repairs were carried out and the show went on. Another occasion when the unusual happened was the first showing of the film 'Dante's Inferno'. In one scene, the Devil was deep in the bowels of the earth, eating a man, with only the lower half of the man's body visible hanging from this huge mouth. The women in the audience were shocked and started stamping their feet and shouting for the film to be stopped. The lights were switched on and Jack Backhouse went on stage and spoke to the audience. The film was replaced by a sort of documentary showing swans swimming around a park lake. This seemed to be acceptable to the women, and it just goes to show how narrow-minded we were in those days'.

In 1936, the interior of the Empire was demolished and it was rebuilt in a modern luxurious style. Its name was changed to the Roxy, and it was re-opened on Christmas Day. Today, there is no cinema in the town. The Co-operative Hall was demolished about 1973, and the Roxy is now a bingo hall.

Although it has proved difficult to determine from local sources when the first Association Football Club was formed in the town, at least one team, Dalton Crusaders, existed in 1906, and was the only Dalton Association Football club playing in the North-Western League. The following year, 1907, Dalton Town F.C.

DOTEN PIKTER PALLAS.

Deer sur,

I was sewer summat spechul hed happen'd as seean as I saa Tommy this week.

He wos girnin' o t'feeace ower, like a Cheshir cat.

An' it wosn't lang befoor he brast out: "What dew ya think on us now, Billy?"

"Nay I dooant kna; what's up now?" ses I.

"What, hevvent ya hard?" ses he, "We've gitten a Pikter Pallas i' Co-op Hall; and a reglar bobby dazzler it is ano!"

"Well, that's nowt t' cra about, is it?" ses I. "What the've hed yan in Barra fer lang enuff!"

"Ah! that's just whar it kums in," ses Tommy. "Our young foaks has been ticed off tel Barra to see ther Elektrik Pikter Pallas. Now tha can stop i' Doton, and see a pikter show ivvery neet, if tha wants; and a gud en ano."

"How dus thou kna?" ses I. "Hes ta bin ta see it, thou ald gad-about?"

"I hev that!" ses Tommy. "An Ise gaain agaan, if I hev ta dew weout a nounce ev bacca for it. It's t' best threepenneth ivver I seed in my life."

"What O!" ses I. "Thous fergitten sen thou telt ma about t' Bell Vew in Manchester!"

"Bell Vew!" ses Tommy. "Bell Vew isn't in it. What, this is too or three Bell Vews rowl'd intel yan. In a nour and a hoaf yer tekhen tel Afrikka, an Amerika, an India, an Lundun, an o ower t' wurld. Ya nivver saa owt like it in yower born days!"

"Ah, but thee dooant fergit," ses I. "as I've bin tel Blakpool, an Duglas, an Manchester, an Lundun, as weel as too er three times on t' Kontinent."

"I dooant kare if ya've bin tel Timbuktoo," ses Tommy. "Ya nivver saa nowt in a nour au a hoaf as al git ower this Pikter Pallas. Now, I've heerd ya toakin about yer strang men; weil, ther wos yan in this show t'tudder neet; he eet sum lifthard bred er summat, an' efter thet he kud karry a seck ev flour just as eesy as if it wos a bag ev fedders. It's terbel stuff is this lifthard bred; this fella just tuk a bite er too, an then he kud lift girt boxes and barrels an things just as eeasy as I kud lift a box ev matches."

"Well, that's nowt," ses I. "I've seen—"

"But howd on," ses Tommy; "I hevvent dun yet; that isnt hoaf ev what ya see. Ya just think yer lukkin throo a girt winda out intel t'wurld, an ya see things happenin' in Afrikka an Amerika just like as if tha wor happenin down in Wellinten -street. Sumtimes ya'll see a fine girt ship cuttin, an cuttin its way throo t'waves. Ya fairly think ya can smell t'soat watter. An t'next minnet t'ship is sinkin befoor yer eyes, an sum foaks esceeap on a raft, an ther tosst about on t'girt waves tel at last ther thraan ontel a dessert iland, an theear tha leev like wild things fer too er three yeers, an ya kan see them hevvin ta feight fer ther lives we reeal leevin lions an tigers. An just when ther gaain ta be wurried up ther frends land up an seeaves them. Well, we've o bin hoddin our breth, expectin ta see them wurried up; an when ther seeaved we o give a girt si, an clap our hands like mad. An ya kan hardly beleev as its nobbut a pikter ya've bin lukkin at. I tell ya, ya nivver saa nowt like it!"

"Just a minnet!" ses I. "Hevvent I telt—"

"But howd on," brast in Tommy agaan. "Let me finish: ya want o' t'toak tel yersel!"

"Now, luk heer!" ses I. But it wos neea use. He wos in again.

"As I was sayin," ses Tommy, "Ya offen toak about yer fine horses—now yons t'pleace ta see sum fine horses, ruffriders, buckjumpers and mountebanks—why sum ev yon cow-boys can ride any sooart ev a horse—even if its a buffalo. Yons yer spot ta gang an see sum fine horsemanship. An then beside o that thers funny pikters as al mek ya laff tel yer badly. An sarius pikters as al mek ya swalla when ya hevent owt in yer mouth; an bla yer nooase when it dussent want it. An as fer t'Co-op Hall, ya'll hardly ken it; its fit up that nice we elektrik leet tel its just like a reglar pallas what ya used ta reed about in t' "Arabian Nights" entertainments. An then thers—"

"Now, now: howd hard," ses I. I hevvent time ta lissen tel any maare; it's about bed time. But if hoaf on its trew as thou ses, an' it meks thee toak like a book, soa as neeaboddy else can git a wurd in, ther mum be summat in it!" ses I.

Soa I hed ta promis Tommy as I wod gang an see it fer mesel, er else he wod hev toakt o neet.

Yowers trewly,

BILLY FAIRPLAY.

were also playing in the same league, with a reserve team in the Ulverston and District League. Dalton Town remained in existence for quite a considerable time; at least until the 1930s. By 1908, Dalton Albion A.F.C. had also appeared on the scene.

It may well have been that this same year also saw the birth of a new team which was to acquire for itself a high reputation in local amateur football, the now legendary Dalton Casuals, or 'Cassies' as they came to be known. One day, almost certainly in 1908, a group of young men met under the copper beech tree at the corner of Station Road and Beckside Road, and decided to form a football club. No-one present at this meeting could have possibly foreseen just how successful the new team would be; but successful it certainly was, and if, at this meeting, anyone had ambitious hopes and aspirations for the proposed team, then they certainly could not have been disappointed with the way things turned out.

With the outbreak of the war in 1914, the Casuals joined the Munitions League, and included in their ranks two second division footballers who had come to Barrow from the Bury area, to work in the shipyard. At the end of the war, in November 1918, they were top of the league having played 8, won 6, drawn 2, lost 0, with 37 goals for and 12 against. The Casuals existed until 1925, when, as a result of financial difficulties caused principally by mismanagement, they were forced to disband.

Without doubt, the most famous person to emerge from the ranks of the Casuals was a local lad, Tommy Johnson, who, at the age of 19, and in the space of only 12 months, leaped from the junior game to the forefront of first class football. At the beginning of the 1918 season he left the Dalton Juniors and played for the Casuals as centre-forward until February 1919, when he joined Manchester City. During his brief stay with the Casuals he scored 42 goals. He also scored in the first match he played for his new club. In his third game for Manchester City, he scored three goals in eight minutes. Later, he was transferred to Everton where he played in the inside-left position to the famous centre-forward, Dixie Dean.

Although the old Casuals faded from the scene in 1925, the name still lives on in the Crooklands Casuals F.C. Founded in 1970 as an offspring of the Dalton Amateur R.L. Club when some of the rugby players also expressed an interest in playing soccer, they played in the Barrow and District Sunday League. Their home ground was the barnfield, situated just behind Langdale Crescent. They had a reasonable degree of success in the first two seasons. The season 1974–5 was a very successful one, winning every game, and the league second division title. At the start of the 1977–8 season, following a long legal battle with the Ministry of Agriculture, they moved to their new home ground, Longlands Park. In 1980, they decided to start a Saturday side, and were founder members of the Furness Premier League. At the present time, the Crooklands Casuals have two Saturday teams and one Sunday team.

Dalton United was founded in 1960, principally by Mr. Fred Caine, who until this time had been actively involved in youth club football. The name for the new club was suggested by Mr. John Knagg. Right from the start they played at Railway Meadow, in the Lancashire League, and have a first and second team.

Dalton Town A.F.C. was started in 1965 by Mr. Harry Asbury, but was originally known as the Newton Lions. No doubt this name can be attributed to the fact that at first the team was based at the Newton public house, noted vendors of Lion Ales. At this time they used the Furness Abbey amphitheatre as their home ground. They play in the Barrow and District Sunday League and now, presumably since it was vacated by the Crooklands Casuals, used the barnfield as their home ground.

Education and Religion

Until 1928, there were five infants and primary schools in the town. It was in this year that the mansion originally built by Mr. G. B. Ashburner and known as Dowdales, was opened as a Central Selective School. Its headmaster was Mr. A. E. Bancroft, M.A., and in its first year it had 224 pupils and 9 members of staff. Over the years it has grown in size, and many alterations have taken place. It is now fully comprehensive, catering for the 11–16 age group. In its Golden Jubilee year (1978), it employed a staff of 60, with 1,060 pupils. It is also the centre for the Evening Institute and an Open University Tutorial Centre and computer facility. On the retirement of Mr. J. T. Franks, B.A., as headmaster in 1976, Mr. M. A. Turner, M.A., succeeded him.

In 1964, approval was obtained from the Department of Education and Science to make a start on the sketch plans for a new school to replace the Green School, which by this time had become badly overcrowded and was completely inadequate. The new Church of England school was opened by the Right Reverend the Lord Bishop of Carlisle on 19 January 1970. Mr. W. E. Hughes was the headmaster until his retirement in 1976, when he was succeeded by Mr. H. Barnes. At present there are 10 members of staff and 220 pupils. The Catholic school on Ulverston Road had also become inadequate for present-day requirements, and on 5 June 1974, their new school, situated at Crooklands on the eastern edge of the town, was officially opened. Its headmaster is Mr. Poole.

The latest school to be built in the town is the George Romney school at Rickett Hills. Although only partly finished, the building was brought into use when the two junior classes from Broughton Road school were transferred here in May 1978. It was not until September 1980 that the remainder of the boys from Broughton Road and all the girls from Nelson Street school were transferred here. Both these schools were closed in July 1980. The opening ceremony was performed by Mr. P. Boulter, Director of Education, on 26 March 1981. A prayer of dedication was said by the Rev. J. P. Inman, and the benediction was given by the Rev. Trevor Park, vicar of Dalton. The headmistress is Mrs. May.

It was probably in 1930 when it was first decided that the town needed a new Sunday school, and on 10 January 1931, the *Dalton News* reported: 'Held for the first time in Furness, at least since mediaeval times, a Consistory Court sat in Dalton Parish Church last Saturday to hear an application by the vicar, the Rev. Trevor Jones, M.A. and the Churchwardens for a faculty regarding the proposed new St Margaret's Sunday School building. Dr. E. B. Pooley was appointed to proclaim the opening of the court in the ancient form: "Oyez, Oyez. Come to the Court. I summon all people who have grievances, complaints or requests to make themselves heard, to make themselves heard"'.

In 1979, after all the legal requirements had been fulfilled, work commenced on the building of a church centre in the ancient graveyard on the south side of the parish church. The inevitable consequence of the digging was that the remains of many former parishioners were disturbed and had to be re-interred. While the construction work was progressing, the nearby grave of George Romney, the artist, was completely restored. The new church centre was opened on 31 October 1980. St Margaret's church on Ulverston Road had been closed for some time, and was purchased by the Catholics who started using it as their parish church in May 1981. Within the last few years, the chapels formerly belonging to the Primitive Methodists and the Baptists have closed and are now used respectively as a potato warehouse and a bakehouse.

Dalton today

On 25 March 1974, the last meeting of the Durban Urban District Council took place, and from this time, the ancient town of Dalton became part of Barrow. This arrangement has never been popular and has caused a good deal of bitter comment, particularly with regard to the fact that Dalton could so easily have acquired Parish Council status at that time but neglected to do so; and at present we still do not have a Parish Council, although recent moves in this direction indicate that we will soon see the birth of the new Dalton Town Council.

According to the 1981 census, the population of the parish of Dalton was 10,939. This suggests that the town itself has a population of approximately 9,000 of whom the greater part are employed outside the town. The principal employers are: in Barrow, Vickers Shipbuilding and Engineering Ltd., Bowater Scott Corporation Ltd., British Cellophane Ltd.; in Ulverston, Glaxochem Ltd.; in Askam, K Shoemakers Ltd. Between them, these firms, and many smaller ones in the area employ well over half the working population of Dalton. It is perhaps rather sad to relate that although government financed advance factory units have been built recently in all the forementioned places, in Dalton there has been none at all. This of course means that the town is permanently deprived of the prestige and prosperity commonly derived from the presence of suitable industry. There is some industry in the town, however, and the principal employers are as follows:

(1) J. S. Blair & Son Ltd., who have a factory at Anty Cross where they manufacture (and also sell) women's foundation garments, lingerie, sportswear and beachwear. They achieved some degree of fame in 1983 when they designed and supplied all the swim suits for the Miss World competition. In 1976, this firm celebrated its centenary, and in a leaflet issued by them to mark the occasion, they describe how a hundred years previously, James Simpson Blair travelled from his native Glasgow to Manchester, with a consignment of whalebone stays which he intended to sell to the Lancashire mill girls. This turned out to be a

highly successful venture, with Mr. Blair delivering his early orders in an old wheelbarrow, which has since become a treasured company heirloom. From this modest beginning, a factory was established in Manchester, and the whole manufacturing side of the business was transferred to Dalton in 1948-9. The firm was taken over by Mr. Ian Rogerson, a Manchester businessman, but recently went into receivership.

(2) Furness Footwear Ltd., who began manufacturing slippers and sandals in 1948, in the old Welfare Centre premises in Broughton Road. The business was established as part of a group of companies based in Bacup. In 1981, in its two factories at Dalton Fields Lane and Long Lane, the firm employed 160 people.

Dalton's long, narrow, winding main street causes severe congestion to traffic passing through the town on the way to and from Barrow, and a few years ago, a group of concerned townspeople, principally young mothers, staged regular protest marches along Market Street in an attempt to persuade the authorities that a by-pass was urgently needed. A possible route was surveyed and then the plans were shelved, partly because of the fact that the undermined condition of the ground to the north of the town would have made the construction of such a road very expensive. Pressure is again mounting, and a typical day's result of a traffic survey carried out by Mr. M. A. Rigden of the Humanities Department, Dowdales School, assisted by 45 pupils, showed that from 8 a.m. to 5 p.m. on Friday, 22 April 1983, vehicles were passing the census point at the rate of 1,077 per hour. At the time of writing, it appears that the government is once again considering the plan.

In 1979, Mr. M. A. Turner, the headmaster of Dowdales school, was instrumental in calling a public meeting to discuss whether or not the town needed a public swimming bath. It was decided that such an amenity was needed, and a committee was elected. To raise money the townspeople were invited to make regular weekly contributions towards the fund, and to date over £200,000 has been raised in this way. A creditable performance by any standards. Construction work on the baths started a few days after the cutting of the first sod on 25 September 1982, by 95-year-old Mrs. Winnie Henderson, the largest single contributor to the fund.

APPENDIX ONE

List of known vicars of the parish of Dalton

1181–1185	. . . . .	Gilbert
1198	. . . . .	William de Horhampt
—	. . . . .	Andrew ?
1243–1277	. . . . .	Robert de Wath
1330	. . . . .	William Cockerham
1369–1370	. . . . .	Thomas Hansey
?	. . . . .	William Golding
1376	. . . . .	John Sharp
1423	. . . . .	Richard Spofforth
1473	. . . . .	Robert Hartyngton
1537	. . . . .	Roger Pele
1551	. . . . .	Roland Wright
1558	. . . . .	Thomas Besbrowne
1573	. . . . .	James Leis
1577	. . . . .	Richard Gardiner
1593	. . . . .	Roger Postlet
1617	. . . . .	William Bowett
1631	. . . . .	Richard Tomlinson
1662	. . . . .	Thomas Whitehead
1663	. . . . .	Anthony Turner
1772	. . . . .	Christopher Cowperthwaite
1823	. . . . .	Joseph Kirkbank
1849	. . . . .	James Morgan
1898	. . . . .	Frank Byard
1905	. . . . .	John G. Leonard
1915	. . . . .	Cuthbert Postlethwaite
1929	. . . . .	Trevor Jones
1939	. . . . .	Roy Sinker
1947	. . . . .	Christopher Cardale
1957	. . . . .	Henry W. Mycroft
1968	. . . . .	George Brassington
1977	. . . . .	Trevor Park

APPENDIX TWO

Nineteenth-Century Dalton Societies

(The titles of all are preceded by the word Dalton).

Amateur Athletic Association (Dalton Harriers) (1906).
Ambulance Brigade. (1899).
Brushing Club.
Cycling Club (1899).
Dialogue Guild.
Golf Club.
Hockey Club.
Horticultural Society (1878).
Literary Society.
May Day Show.
Morris Tube Rifle Club (1906).
Music Festival and Eisteddfod (1897).
Nursing Association.
Orchestral Society.
Ornithological Society.
Philharmonic Society.
Poultry & Pigeon Society.
Poultry Protection Society.
Rose Society.
Shorthand Writers' Association.

The political clubs referred to were the Conservative Club, which was opened in the presence of a large gathering, on Saturday, 19 March 1887, and the Liberal Club, which opened its premises in Hall Street on 8 January 1897. The latter remained active until about 1947, when the premises were purchased by the Baldwin Masonic Hall Company Ltd. The Conservative Club was originally situated in Station Road, in what is now the Dalton Baths Fund Shop. The opening ceremony was performed by Mr. W. G. Ainslie, M.P., and Mr. Edward Wadham and Mr. Godby were elected as chairman and secretary respectively. In 1914 the club moved to its present home

APPENDIX THREE

Twentieth-Century Dalton Societies

The Dalton Book Club (1764)   Secretary: Mr. R. Porter
The Dalton Horticulture Society (1878) Secretary: Mr. L. Crossley
The Dalton Folk Dance Group (1927)   Secretary: Mrs. D. Laisby
The Dalton Bridge and Chess Club (1931?) Secretary: Mr. W. Gilchrist
The Dalton Local History Society (1975) Secretary: Mrs. V. Phillipson
The Dalton and District Civic Society (1980) Secretary: Mrs. Jan Matthews
The Dalton Flower Club (1980)   Secretary: Stella Coulthard
The Dalton Society of Artists (1980)   Secretary: Mrs. C. Barr

APPENDIX FOUR

Places of historic interest

Dalton Castle   (226739). 14th-century pele tower. Now a museum. Curator: Mr. Ivan Whitehead, 18 Market Place.

Furness Abbey   (218718). 1127–1537. History as described in Chapters 2 and 3. May be reached by car. Signposted from the Barrow–Dalton road. Admission via museum near car park.

High Haume   (226760). Possible site of Hougun. Remains of beacon. Access from Dalton–Askam road. East from Greenhaume farm then north via footpaths.

Holy Well   (216747). Site of ancient spring, at one time supplying piped water to nearby monastic buildings. Little remains to be seen today.

Little Mill   (221729). Site and some remains of. One of the abbey mills. Continued in use until the 19th century. Part of the mill dam and also the ancient road to Mill Brow are still visible. Access from Low Road footpath.

Marsh Grange   (Not on map). Ancient farm. Existed as early as 1252. Originally known as Stephengarth. Became a monastic possession. Home of Sir Hugh Askew after the dissolution. Birthplace of Margeret Askew who married Judge Thomas Fell of Swarthmoor Hall in 1632, and subsequently George Fox, founder of the Quaker movement, in 1669. Private property. Access from the Ireleth–Kirkby road.

Pinfold   (226738). Stone-built circular enclosure for stray cattle. Situated on Goose Green. Age uncertain, but certainly pre-1825.

St Helen's Chapel   (218745). Believed to be a Chapel of Ease dating from the monastic era. Now a ruin. Situated in the field between St Helen's farm and the Dalton–Roanhead road.

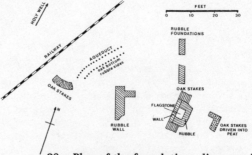

28.   Plan of the foundations discovered at Chapel Meadow in 1801.

Tytup Hall   (236759). Early 18th century, but replacing an older building on same site, possibly Orgrave Hall. Thomas West wrote *Antiquities of Furness* while living here in 1774–5. Access by appointment, from Holmes Green–Lindal road.

NOTES

Chapter One — The Early History

1. Anciently 'Forness', meaning 'fore' or further promontory.
2. The route the Romans would almost certainly have taken to enter Furness, if any.
3. Collingwood, W. G., *Saga Book of the Viking Club*.
4. From the Danish *arvol*, meaning inheritance ale.

Chapter Two — The Middle Ages

1. Possibly derived from *Bekan* (personal name) and *gill* (a valley with a stream).
2. *Soc*: privilege of holding a court for the administration of justice.
3. *Sac*: judicial privileges over tenants and vassals.
4. *Tol*: tax on wheat ground in the lord's mill and on similar transactions.
5. *Theam*: power to try bondmen and villeins.
6. *Infangentheof*: jurisdiction over thieves apprehended within the manor.
7. This price may have varied over the years.
8. This figure is based on the fact that five centuries later the population was only just over 600.
9. Some point between the dissolution of the monastery in 1537 and the great plague of 1631–2.
10. Originally this court was held on 13 October.
11. *C. & W. Proceedings*, New Series, vol. 10.
12. *Furness Past and Present*, vol. 2, p. 49.
13. Although there were many outbreaks of plague in the Middle Ages, this is the only epidemic correctly referred to as the Black Death.

Chapter Three   Tudor and Stuart Dalton

1. *See* Barnes, *Barrow and District*, pp. 39–41, for further details.
2. He had already secretly married Anne Boleyn in January 1533.
3. Although this assessment was welcomed by the farmers, it was challenged in 1583, when Queen Elizabeth's Attorney-General, John Brograve, obtained a lease of the provisions which had previously been paid to the monastery, and demanded that he should now receive them. The tenants successfully opposed this claim in the Chancery of the Duchy of Lancaster on 7 June 1583, thus permanently establishing their rights and discouraging further claims.
4. This is despite a severe plague in 1597. There is evidence that after a natural catastrophe such as this, contrary to what one might expect, the birthrate actually increases, and over a period of five years would tend to absorb the effects of one year's high mortality.
5. There are always exceptions. West informs us that Henry Kelley of Dalton died aged 116 in 1720.

Notes--*continued*

Chapter Four — The Emergence of the Modern Town

1. *Furness & the Industrial Revolution*, pp. 193, 206.
2. This information concerning the environs of the castle was published in *Trans. C. & W.A.A.Soc.*, New Series, vol. X.
3. *The Making of the English Landscape.*
4. *Barrow News*, 25 November 1977.
5. Roberts, *Directory of Barrow & District.*
6. *Universal British Directory*, 1798.
7. North Lonsdale Licensing List.
8. Mannex, *History & Directory of Barrow*, 1876.
9. Bulmer and Rooney, *Furness & West Cumberland.*
10. Runes: symbols or letters of the earliest Germanic alphabet. Widely used by Scandinavians and Anglo-Saxons.
11. *Dalton Local Board — Accounts.*

BIBLIOGRAPHY

Baines, E., *A History of the County Palatine and Duchy of Lancaster* (1870), Vol. 2, pp. 647-51.

Barber, H., *Furness and Cartmel Notes* (1894).

Barfoot and Wilkes, *Universal British Directory* (1798).

Barnes, F., *Barrow & District*, 2nd Edn. (1978).

Barrow Naturalists' Field Club, Annual Reports (1902-4), Vol. 17.

Beck, T. A., *Annales Furnesienses* (1844).

Bulmer, T., *History & Directory of Furness & Cartmel* (1911).

Close, W., *Itinerary of Furness and Its Environs* (1813).

Cumberland and Westmorland Antiquarian and Archaeological Society, *Transactions* (1884-5), Vol. 8, Old Series; (1910), Vol. 10, New Series.

Gaythorpe, H., *Furness Lore* (1880-82), Vol. 3.

Mannex, P., *History & Directory of Furness & West Cumberland* (1882).

Marshall, J. D., *Furness & the Industrial Revolution* (1958).

Marshall, J. D. and Walton, J. K., *The Lake Counties* (1981).

North Lonsdale Magazine (1822), Vol. 3; (1900-2), Vol. 4.

Page, W., *Victoria History of the County of Lancaster*, Vol. 8, pp. 304-19.

Parson, W., and White, W., *History, Directory & Gazetteer of the Counties of Cumberland & Westmorland* (1829).

Richardson, J., *Furness Past & Present* (1880), Vol. 2.

Romney, J., *Memoirs of the Life & Works of George Romney* (1830).

Tyson, J., *Dalton-in-Furness District Local Board — Accounts* (1882-96).

West, T., *Antiquities of Furness* (1774).

West, T., *Antiquities of Furness*, Edn. Close (1805).

INDEX

LIST OF SUBSCRIBERS

Maxine St. L. Hayes
E.J. Hearsey
James Helling
Mrs Anne Hemsley
Mrs Win Henderson
Jack Heptinstall
Geoffrey Holme
D. & M.W. Holmes
Dr. J.E. Horrocks
Mr & Mrs J.T. Huddleston
R.N. Hudson
D. & J. Hurst
William J. Iddon
Mr & Mrs Ian Inglis
Yvonne Inman
John I. Ireland
Elizabeth Jackson
S.M. Jackson
David J. Jackson
J.F.B. Jackson, C.B.E., F.R.S.A.
Annie B. Johnson
D. Johnson
Fred Johnson
Christopher D. Jones
J.R. Jones
Pauline Jones
Harry Kellett
W.R. Kendall
P.S. Kenley
A.W. Kilburn
M. Kirkby
Daniel Jeffrey
Helen H. Kitchin
T.H. Kneebone
D.W. Kydd
P. Laird
Mr & Mrs Robert Lander
Marjorie Lanworn
Patricia Latimer
Miss Sandra Lawton
Jack Lindsay
Mrs Kathleen Lister
D. Lumb
D.G.B. Lyon
Andrew M. McAdam
Miss F.M. McDougall
Christine McEneaney
A. & A. McFadzean
J. McFadzean
J. Simeon Manwaring
J.I & L. Marsden
Prof. G.H. Martin
John J. Martin, B.A.
J. Melling
J. Milburn

F.E. & V.J. Mitchell
N. Moneypenny
Mrs Sylvia J. Morrison
Mr & Mrs J.W.F. Morton
Frank Murray
Kenneth Murray
Brian P. Neatis
W.D. & M. Noall
Clifford Norton
R. O'Brien
Brian Otto
Revd. Trevor Park
Kenneth S. Parker
Andrew & Neil Parkin
W. T. Pearson
J.M. Phillipson
Leslie S. Phillpotts
Olive Pickavance
Colin Pickthall
H.D. & O.M. Pilkington
Mrs Nora Pilling
Mrs Sandra Pitkeathly
Revd. Alan Postlethwaite
G. & M. Postlethwaite
L.C.R. Thom-Postlethwaite
Stephen Postlethwaite
Andrew Poulsen
Mrs Margaret Preston
Roger L. Preston
W. Procter
P.P. Quiggin
Christine Quirk
T. Quirk
William A. Quirk
William H. Quirk
Terry Raine
Capt. J.L. Randall, M.A. (Oxon)
Ashley Raven
Fred Rawlinson
J.A. Rhodes
Elaine P. Richardson
Ralph Rigg
James F. Roberts
Mrs K.R. Roberts
A.I. Robinson
W.H. Robinson
Dr. William Rollinson
Mrs V. Round
Kevin Routledge
Frances Rowland
Kevin Rowley
Miss May S. Rule
R.G. Savage
Julie Sharp

Mr & Mrs R. Simpson
Peter W. Skellon
A.E. Slater
Henry A. Slater
Ian & Jean Smith
Isabel Clague-Smith
Maureen Smith
Michele Smith
Paul Smith
G.I. Spencer
Alan Steele
David J. Stewart
Revd. & Mrs Christopher
Strong
T.V. Sykes
Robert B. Sylvester
Jack A. Taylor
John C. Taylor
Joseph Taylor
Mr & Mrs M. Taylor
Thomas S. Telfer
Dorothy Thompson
John W. Thompson
Marjorie Thorburn
Mr & Mrs R. Thornton
F.J. & M. Thurman
Raymond Tubman
E. Travis
J.H. Turner
John E.R. Ullock
Mrs Margaret Ullock
Gilbert Uren
Miss C. Walker
Stanley Walmsley
John N. Walton
Moyra Walton
Peter M. Walton
Stephen J. Walton
T.A. Walton
Leslie Wardle
M. & W. Warwick
Robert Wearing
Mrs Isabel Wharton
W.P. Whiteley
J. Whittam
Mr & Mrs T. Wight
Jonathan Wignall
J.D.J. Wildridge
Harold Wilkes
Andrew F. Wilson
Harry Wilson
R.R. Woodend
E. Wren
R.A. Yorke